RUNOFF

D1567456

Clay Matthews

BlazeVOX [books]

Buffalo, New York

Runoff by Clay Matthews

Copyright © 2009

Published by BlazeVOX [books]

Printed in the United States of America

Book design by Geoffrey Gatza

First Edition
ISBN: 9781935402695
Library of Congress Control Number 2009910012

BlazeVOX [books]
303 Bedford Ave
Buffalo, NY 14216

Editor@blazevox.org

publisher of weird little books

BlazeVOX [books]

blazevox.org

2   4   6   8   0   9   7   5   3   1

B   X

Endless thanks to the states of Oklahoma, Missouri, Mississippi, and all others mentioned; the four seasons of the years 2007 and 2008; Geoffrey Gatza for all the work that he's done and continues to do, and for taking a chance on this beast; Nate Pritts, Matt Hart, Brandi Homan, and Jon Thrower for their help, friendship, and reads; my family for always, always being there; and, above all, Jan Matthews, for her inspiration, love, and everything else.

A year is an amazing thing.

Table of Contents

RUNOFF

I. GROUNDSKEEPERS

I sit on the bench and feed the stray dog a bit of raw meat,
because I like it when the blood drips off the fang.
Down the road a local tavern is holding a turkey shoot, where men
will come out from the hills with small guns and large guns, and try
to make a shotgun pattern into something constrained, something tight,
something with a pattern in it that tells the story of beauty, death, mastery—
life's constant elusive treasures. Ammo and alcohol: these are one way
to get through a Saturday. The puddles have grown large, the lakes
have grown larger, and the oceans are swallowing ice as if hung over.
We who used to prospect on gold are now prospecting on forever,
or the future, the water level, the temperature, and sometimes at last
can almost see ourselves from space, as only one place on a very long list
of other places. If there's going to be a story here I'm not going
to control it. No demands, no because I said so's. Only a drink
in my hand or nothing and why, why, why. I am hiding today
in the stacks at the local library, I am hiding downtown, I am hiding
east of town, on a park bench, with a stray dog who has almost
entered the state of mange, but as of yet still looks like he could be
rescued. We can all be rescued. The point of life is to keep believing
that. It may be a myth, but we are the creatures of myth. The other
animals tell stories of us, how we rose from the earth, fought with
the earth, surrendered ourselves and our dead to the earth, and wept
and wept. A July funeral and humid enough to take your breath away.
But the breath was gone then, the breath had left for a little while
anyway, as it does, everyday, while we unconsciously go about asking
it back. Come home. Please. Such a sweet little word and so hard
to say no to. I am hiding out at the local Elks Club, I am hiding out
in a caboose by a swing set, and the children shall never make me leave.
One-day, two-day, huckleberry blue. The river is rising, come back
to the raft, honey. And in the water wild toothéd beasts of the deep:
channel cat, alligator gar, the sight of each reflected in the haunted bead
of sweat your mother rubbed off your forehead at night. In one direction,
Mississippi, in another, Missouri, and Tennessee, Arkansas, Kentucky, Illinois
all bordering the same nightmares, the same dreams, the same hopes all told
in the odd phrasing of state mottos, of state birds, of state trees that blossom
or do not blossom or hardly even grow anymore at all. I read that Faulkner
would not allow air conditioning in his home, and that on the day
after his death his wife bought and installed a new window unit, turned it on
and just stood for a time in front of the cold breeze. In the summer months, we are
of the summer months. We are sticky and wet and moving inside and out.
I've known people to spend whole days in Wal-Mart just to cool off, and all day
watch as others come in with wet shirts, and leave carting big cardboard boxes
of the American dream as climate control, or the boxes of giving in—

a season of cheap dinners and no movies, of sitting all together in the one room
where the machine hums, until it's cold enough they're putting blankets
on their legs, staring outside at the sun. Go on, go on. A summer anthem.
The blanket itself. It has come down upon us. It has risen. And the mosquitoes
haunt the backyard, the legs, the space between collar and hair, dawn
and dusk, hovering, blood-thirsty, tiny, flying fangs. And fan and fandango. Blow them
all down. They can slip right into your hand, and you won't even feel it, until later,
and an itch and a welp and a curse against nature. We're all cursed. We're cursing
ourselves. We're cursing the fucking universe and doesn't it feel right
to do so, sometimes. There is the expletive. There is abundance. We are
overflowing, we are not enough, I am not enough but I want to be more,
I am trying to be more but I keep getting in the way of myself, or others
are in the way of myself. Live free or die, and one of those is bound to come
true. I've a friend who has the first leg of the proposition tattooed on his arm,
because the first carries the living part, and to live is to live the unknown.
And to die is, also, to die the unknown. And we die and we die our hair
and our shirts, and my mother goes out with scissors and comes back
with a bouquet of English lace, throwing them into water, dying the water red, then
watching as the color climbs up the stem and takes over the white. You could say of this
that nature is in a search for balance. You could say of this that the water
will take us all in the end. You could say that it's beautiful to watch a flower
go from white to pink to red on a kitchen table. You could watch a cut thing
just fighting to stay alive. But we can't help ourselves, or sometimes don't
want to. It is within the nature of each man to be capable of terrible things.
I say this as one, and speak for us all, which is admittedly a terrible thing itself.
We are all capable of so much: beautiful things, awful things, things of both
beauty and awe. In the summer of the slug, we set out bowls of beer each night,
a drink of beer for the self, a pour in the ground for the departed, and the rest
in a pool for what slithers in the dark. If you were patient, you could watch
as they slowly came toward the smell, then up the side, then in, drinking
and rolling, and rolling and drinking, up, and over, and down and down
until they were dead. By each morning five or six had drank themselves into
bloated corpses, never knowing when to stop, or how to stop, or else just not
wanting to stop, to keep going perhaps knowing that this was a good way to go.
We may say slugs have no consciousness of their death. We may say summer
has no consciousness of its heat. But I say they do. So it has been said,
and whether it is true or not is irrelevant, it is true by my own definition of truth,
meaning right, and terrible, and unavoidable and everything in the world
we all want to hold together, everything that is impossible to do so. This is going
well, I think, turn over the tape and tomorrow we'll pick-up where we've left off.
An interview. A question. Use whatever you want because I know my words
will end up twisted into something else. Or else something with legs, something
with wings, the words gone to paper, folded, and folded again, the words
as origami and you as the person who knows a thing or two about origami.
Take flight, little white crane. Past the wide river, over the swamplands, down

into the low branches of a Cypress tree. And the Cypress grows thick and dark,
and hides the secrets of humankind, the secrets the animals tell each other
of humankind, the myths they make up and the myths that are not myths at all.
I saw this in a dream once: a big woman in a wig who, when taking the wig off,
became water, and flooded the door, then the kitchen. At the back of my house
the water will not leave the basement alone. I built a small levee, and the water went over.
I built a larger levee, and the water went under. I dig the dirt and I curse
the dirt and I curse the water and the never-ending rain. The rain giveth,
the rain taketh away. Away it runs down the good levees and the bad levees,
and the people sit on levees in lawn chairs and drink as the water rises,
and the people sit in houses shadowed by levees and drink as the water rises,
and the people sit on their hands on park benches a county away and drink
as the water rises. And the summer comes, and the crops come, and the wheat
grows thick and the corn grows tall, and taller, but it is all too wet to cut.
And so a town bustles a little, and a farmer buys a new pair of pants, say
a dress for his woman, new shoes for his children, or maybe, more, the lumber
for a new barn, a new combine, pivot, new, new, new, new. Because in the beginning
the rain was good. But now it has become something more, something evil,
or another structure for which we are able to supply names like good and evil
and mean them to their curséd roots. In the backyard enough food to feed
a county, going green, then under, then old, then done. And nothing to do
but shake your head, wipe your brow, slap the mosquitoes off your arms
and sleep at night, or not sleep at night, or wake-up to the light silhouette
of a ghost in the other room, taking back the shades and opening a window.
The heat rises and the turtles bake themselves slowly on the logs, or the edge
of ditches, or, for the wild ones, the highway. The highway that comes
and goes, the highway that eats turtles, and turtle shells, and armadillos and deer
and dogs and children and grown men riding on eighteen wheels. Eighteen wheels,
and a bed of roses. Flowers on the side of the road, a field of crosses marking
so many deaths, or potential deaths, or a field of crosses just as a political statement.
And graveyards are political statements, too. There is Marxism in a graveyard,
and communism, and Christianity, and democracy, and fascism, etc. The graves
themselves as markers of class, identity, religion, and so forth. The coffins
as an underground extension of the visible. But inside the coffins we are all
the same. And when the water rises we are the same, and when it takes us under
we are the same, and, in a puddle of blood on the side of the road we are the same,
we rot when rot and we stink when we rot and the maggots do not lie.
So keep cool, because the summer comes. Keep cool, because the heat will take you
down. A long day of slow work, a stubborn resistance to hydration, and somewhere
right now in the world someone is dying of heat exhaustion, or exhaustion in general,
and so on. So I take myself to the grocery store, and buy bags of ice, and coolers,
and drinks, and put the ice on the drinks and in my cup and on my forehead,
and remember Ellis, an enormous man I used to work with, who would hold the ice
against the artery in his wrist, using his blood like a central a/c unit. Or else he would
tie the ice up in a bandana on the back of his neck, and again, find the blood,

and let it go cold. Hot and cold—these are undeniable binaries. But if you push
either end far enough it's just a tingle, and then a twitch, and then long, slow breaths
into whatever comes next. So the turtles come and go, and move through the front
yard, at a turtle's pace, while somewhere else a snake is paying the price for being written
up in a book long ago. My great-grandfather could catch a snake by the tail, swing it
in the air, and at its furthest point crack it like a whip, sending the head flying off
into the distance. Because a snake is mythical the head must be separated from the body,
or else it may live forever, mangled and ruptured as it might be. I was asked
the other day if I was writing about the end of the world. My answer: all poems
are Armageddon poems, and if not, they should be, or will be in time. Summer is
sometimes a time machine itself. Or not summer itself but summer moments,
when grabbing a cold beer or cold bottle of wine, when sitting with the June bugs
in the dark, or seeing a Roman candle go off in the air, for one instant you are
transported back to another place, or a future place, or else you are at last exactly
in the current moment of being. I worked once for a man who sold fireworks,
and ran a fireworks stand, and made very good money ripping off the lower classes
with cheap cardboard and black powder. But a bang is something, and an oooohhh,
and an aaaahhhh, and lights in the sky are something, and putting the lights there
is an art, or else it should be, or will be, or could be. At this year's local fireworks show,
I watched as the fire made a weeping willow out of the sky, and a flag, and one firework
contained a heart, but for some reason the man letting them off sent the heart up
upside down. I don't know what this means. It was an accident, surely, but is anything really
an accident. Perhaps and perhaps not, or maybe it was just the humidity in the air
doing with the cosmos as it liked. In another field beside a road, a small graveyard.
So many graves, some coming at you out of nowhere. Once I was walking through
a field of wild flowers, the thistle thick, plum bushes, and tripped over an unmarked
place where the old people had laid an older person long ago. There is no metaphor
for this story, no allegory, no point, no symbol, only that I cherished the stone
for a moment, and the place, and the colors of nature and the wildness of nature
and the immanence of so many things. It was as if I was of the earth
and had come back to the earth, but in the distance a pair of power lines hummed,
and pulled me back to the rope going home, the wire back, the electricity that runs
through us all. What an odd sensation to throw a rock and feel something
in the shoulder spark, I have felt this, like a tiny firework going off inside.
The cosmos of the body. The cosmos of gunpowder. The cosmos of a single field
of wild flowers, where the roots tangle underneath, and the bugs gnaw
on the roots, and the worms do, too, and the birds come for both, and I come
to say something about them all. So I'm a gossip, of the worst sort or best sort.
Don't start me talking, I'll tell everything I know. The great return. The great pretender.
The spider webs coming each morning, just outside the door, to hold you a moment
in their spiteful and sticky grip, their trickery of light and absence of light,
grabbing you before you wander off, out into the world of more spiders
and more webs and more trickery. Magic. Abracadabra. And corporate webs,
and spider accounts, and an entire monopoly of commerce just trying to act natural.
Act natural: what an impossible thing to do. But we try, because we have to, because

we don't know how to, or how not to, because all the world's a stage, as it was said
before. And summer is a stage, too, and its magic, its method, its lack of method,
its madness. Mad summer days spent in the junkyard, breaking windows
in old cars from the sixties, I tell you sometimes it feels good to be destructive.
Anger comes in strange forms and at strange times. I spent an entire afternoon
with my mother smashing flower pots against a wooden fence at the house
my grandfather had built when young, this was just weeks before we would move out.
And it was summer then, and it is always summer when in the summer, when of it.
And always winter when in winter, with the mind of winter, etc. But the cold and snow
has no relevance to me now—only what is, what I am, what I've become, am becoming,
good, bad, ugly, or indifferent. But not indifferent. Not indifferent! I am hiding out
in the patio furniture, I am hiding out from myself. I am hiding out beside a small creek
used as a dump site. And washing machines, and dryers, and the skeletons of worn-out
lawnmowers. The water takes it all in and away. The earth takes it down, and down.
We are digging to China. We are digging to hell. We are digging through the igneous layer
and beyond—there is something under us all. And watch your step by the electric fence
else it shock you into believing in borders and property. No trespassing, they'll shoot you
on site, where you stand, as if they were aiming for your shadow. This is not making sense
anymore, this is an impression, or digression. This is the theme of summertime to me,
where the livin's easy. But it's not easy. It's never easy anymore. There are lakes
and pontoons on the lakes and people in pontoons with jet skis and loud music
and chicken-salad sandwiches wrapped in sandwich bags and chips and soda and beer
and this is what it is because it is easy, for a little while, anyway. The great escape.
Plan yours well. Plan it today. They will not let you leave for long they will come for you
and they will find you they will interrogate you they will go through your home
they will ask you about your dreams your alibis your motives and torture you
and burn your wrists with small votives. A candle for the heat. Citronella for the mosquitoes.
We humans are an intelligent bunch of creatures, but nothing can slow the rise of the bug
when it wants to come up, when it is thirsty in the heat, when the water stands
and they feel like making love. On, on, and on. And on the roads, the signs to tell us
where to go, and how far to get there: Oklahoma City – 72 miles, Tulsa – 72 miles,
and here you are in the middle of everything. Robertson's Ham Sandwiches
and The Jesse James Wax Museum, and other small museums and the homes
of Will Rogers and Laura Ingalls Wilder and a church around Joplin or Springfield
where you can be married in the Precious Moments Chapel. Isn't life precious!
Isn't it all, and wax, and of the museum, the minute, the catalog, the yes and no or
I agree and/or disagree. Tomorrow they're building a new highway. And the day after
that, and the day after that, and the day after that. It's going on, or going over
an older one, or going from two-lane to four-lane, or concrete to asphalt, but it is
June or July and they are making plans to get us there. Or, getting us there. Outta here.
Or we're getting ourselves there all on our own. Driving while some crop duster comes low
across the road, and under the power lines, the sprayers stopping in perfect synchronicity
with the edge of one field and the beginning of another, heading straight for a tree
line and then back up into the blue, and down, and loud, engines blaring. And I stick
my head out in the sun and watch, and smell the pesticide, and take it in to my lungs.

And breathe in, and breathe out. Breathe in, breathe out. Deeply, and the doctor
with the cold stethoscope on your chest, your back, your whole entire future resting
in two small lines running up to his ears. Can you hear it beat? Can you hear
the phlegm? Can you hear the frustration/joy/beast/hope/hate/love/etc. crawling within?
And outside the beasts crawl through the field, a raccoon with a broken leg,
finding a small comfort in a watermelon busted open by the heat or the birds.
Pink flesh, broken flesh. Black seeds in the way of what we'd most like to get at.
Black seeds as the future manifestation of what we'd like to get at again.
But doesn't the circle of life go on. I take up the manure and put it on the rose bush.
And the rose bush takes the manure and gives me roses. And thorns, too, and leaves,
and shade, going up over the trellis and onto the other side. Dogwood, azalea,
cherry, maple. Grow, blossom, be trees, and be good trees. I am benevolent these days,
sometimes, sometimes I am not. I would prefer to try and be honest with you,
but believe me, there are some things I think you would rather not know. Driving, driving,
outside an old gas station, I read their latest message to the world on a white marquee:
Happiness is having neither too much nor not enough. So many things in the world to wrap
one's head around. Happiness, what is it, is it that, I'd never have known. So consider
the happy man, is he really happy, or has he learned to act happy, or been told to act happy,
or grown tired of those that would ask: Why in the world aren't you happy? It's what
we all want for each other, what we rarely find ourselves, or what we often find
ourselves, but can't hold onto, can't keep, can't pet on the head while it curls
around our legs and drops to nap on the ground. That's a good dog. Bad dog.
The dog that just won't listen to a word I say. Summer, summer, summer. And some of her.
But not all of her. Or else, all of her. I can't say. I don't know. You don't say. Get it.
Got it. And I got it bad. Driving a county road and the irrigation pivots toward the west,
back to the east, spraying the corn and at one point coming down in buckets on the road,
so much so that I pull over, open the door, and walk out into the mist, and then the wet,
and then the water coming down like wild rain—hard, strong, cold, well water. And the corn
stands proud so I stand proud, and feel alive, and wish I could always feel this way,
but it would kill you to always feel this way, it would break your heart to always feel
this way, it would be what a teacher once told me a constant orgasm would be: terrible,
terrible, a never-ending hell. But is that so? We'll never know, we are not allowed to know,
and so we feel by difference, we love by difference, we act by difference, are by difference,
note by difference the bird with the orange chest and red chest, the bird with the scissor-tail
and no tail at all, the drake, the hen, the pretty ducks on the pond. Shh, shh, shh, shh,
and the water from the pivot hushes us into another moment of contentment. How to be
one with everything and not go the route of the hippies, down into too much love
and then drugs and then out on the other side in anger and hate and frustration. You've got
politics, man, use them. And outside the windows and in the fields the surveyors with their
magical white boxes on stilts, looking out at the world for a long time, and seeing things
I have never seen, or things I have seen from a perspective I have never seen, we shall
none of us ever see through the same perspective. This is what makes life beautiful This is
what makes life difficult, and impossible, and constant and just goddamn heartbreaking.
And a man is eating tacos somewhere, with good, roasted pork, the best kind of pork,
carnitas on corn tortillas. And across the state, or in another state, a woman takes

the first sip of a margarita, the rocky salt just resting on her top lip, the sweet and sour, and lime. And if you put these two together you'd have a photo op for a vacation south of the border. But these are all photo ops, and they are together whether they know it or not, and they do, somewhere, know it, somehow, as the dimensions go on, and time goes on, and on, and onward, until somewhere they stop, and rest there together for a while, and sit and look not at each other but out, across a great field, down the mountain, up from the valley. It is ups and downs sometimes and sometimes just flat as far as the eye can see. And here is where one could watch a sunset, or a sunrise, depending on which is preferred—the yawn awake or the yawn asleep, getting under the covers or waking in a light sweat, and pulling the covers back off to reveal another day. Festivities of the season. Funnel cakes and fried fish sandwiches. Prom queens and drag queens and queens of the broken hearts. And just outside town on Saturday nights, the local drag races, an amateur event, full of hope and fuel concocted in a portable rental shed sitting in the barren back yard. Mustangs, GTOs, Camaros, etc.: muscle and a quarter mile. And though it would not appear it there is sound and speed and science here, these are everywhere, what they say the world is made of, these are nowhere, these are myths just as the flying man is a myth. But a myth we work toward, to become, by machine, by aviation, by the big yellow wings of a crop duster coming down and buzzing a shadow into your heart, a fear, a dream, a memory of when as a child you stood on the top bunk and thought happy thoughts, and jumped, and held still in the air for a minute. But it was not a minute, not even a second, but more, too, now as you look back, you look at yourself stuck in the air, but this is not you anymore it's me, I'm there, flying, just inches from the ceiling, the floor and rug and reality miles and miles below. Dreams and the stories of dreams. Outside a turtle moves through the grass, slowly, as turtles do, and it has no recollection of running against rabbits, no hopes to run against rabbits, no philosophy on rabbits at all. Or else it does, or else it is an alternate version to one story, now two stories, flowing along beside each other like rivers, and they are rivers, moving at separate speeds sometimes, sometimes the same speeds, and even sometimes they come back together to be one for a moment, to be beast and beast, angel and angel, two wild creatures still going wild. And the turtle wakes up one day and turns over, and we have the world. We build a home on the turtle's back. We plant wheat on the turtle's back. We take a jeep out with a cooler full of beer on the turtle's back, and drive up, over each ridge, each bump of the shell that perhaps provides extra structure, or support, or perhaps is just the turtle's way of supplying beauty to itself. For beauty need have no function. This is an old way of saying an old thing. Sitting in a lawn chair in east Kentucky with a jar of moonshine brewed at nearly seventy-percent alcohol, drinking what we can get down, and the stars and coming sound of crickets. I could holler right now. I will holler. Because a holler is the summer's way of letting it out, it is the summer anthem. And there is no echo that I can hear but there is echo somewhere. At some point, long after I am dead, my voice will bounce off a star somewhere, and keep moving, and come back, and perhaps in the distance of the future you will hear it again, as a wild, loud whoop wakes you in the middle of the night. Sometimes we mistake our own voices brought back from the cosmos as ghosts. Sometimes we mistake ghosts for our own voices, our own weight on the floor, the fault of our own eyes looking upon a shadow as it passes beside the bed at night, and stands for a moment until we blink and it's gone, our eyes shuttered into another dimension. Because you can never open your eyes and see the same thing again. This is a trick we play on ourselves. It is changing. It is always changing. And in the summer it changes rapidly—the water rises, the water dries out. The grass grows thick and green and lush, and then brown, and then not at all. From one day to the next the mosquito lives and the mosquito dies. But the mosquito, in the summertime, will persist. And we will persist. Though not all of us, as on those first hot days we lose a few to the heat, because of old age or young age or middle age and too much courage or pride. In a house down the street, walking the other day, I saw over their fence that they had built a small bar for a porch, with Christmas lights strung around the deck, bar stools, and even a few beer signs tacked up behind it. What we can't get out to we bring home. Or else, home is where the heart is. Or else many of us have our heart wound up in a glass, or not a glass but the beauty glass makes, the ease of it, its smoothness, that even when it shatters it doesn't seem to mind, but only becomes sharp as if to say All these years I have warned you—I am more fragile than you ever really knew. So there is a joy in breaking glass if we do it on our own—glass against a concrete wall, beer bottles busted with a baseball bat. But when the glass breaks by accident it is sad, an uncontrollable sad, and it sits there, broken, for what is then one small version of eternity—nobody walking, nobody moving, everyone just looking down to see the extent of the damage, the distance to which this object has stretched out, the big pieces and the small pieces, a little chunk of memory later pulled out of the heel. So glass and porches, lights and buzzers. The porch, the mascot of summer. Screened-in or opened, the old porches, set-up by the old minds of architects with no a/c themselves, structured to pull in the summer breeze. Because when the summer breeze comes there is nothing better than the summer breeze, it is a promise of heaven, it is promise itself, god on your face for a moment if you believe in god, the hands of a woman you love on your face if you believe in love, and if you believe in nothing, then it is nothing at its full potential, nothing pushed in your direction and relaxing the great trembling nothing that goes beating in your nothing of a soul. So one provided the porch. And one brought the hush-puppies. And one brought the coleslaw and one brought the corn bread and one brought the fried chicken and another the pie. And drinks and music and plates and paper towels, forks and knives and napkins. Feed us. Or else we'll feed each other. No matter how you try you still cannot stop the world from spinning round. It is the spinning in the larger sense that brings summer back. It brings everything back, it swings out and it swings in again. And I don't know what we are. I don't know what I am, or who I am, exactly, or who I want to be. Sometimes it feels like a wind carries me. Sometimes it feels like I am the wind itself. Sometimes I am just moved to peace by a summer breeze. Or moved to remember, or recollect, or moved to happiness at what I have, sorrow at what I don't have, sometimes I sing, sometimes I shout, sometimes I tremble and sometimes I shiver. And the earth quakes. I've felt if before. A small shake and a few cans fell from the pantry, and a picture off the wall of my ancestors standing with each other on the stairs, wearing hats and white clothes and other manifestations of the season. One day the hush-puppies were seasoned well. One day they were not. These are, after all, the days of good and bad hush-puppies. And sunburns and suntans. The human skin going red, going brown, deep brown, sweet brown, a brown I would like to hold into the colder days of winter. But this is not about winter nor about white. Only white shirts, white hats, white skirts,

white skin going either red or brown or olive or freckled but going somewhere away
from white. And on the back patio they were putting lemon in their hair, and braiding
it, and singing rhymes they sang as children while jumping rope. And though the rope
is gone they can still hear it skipping in their heads, all of them at once, the same rope
manifesting itself between them, hitting brick and hitting brick and hitting brick.
Then one goes inside, and they all go inside, and they are jumping there together,
spinning and clapping hands. I'm off for a while in the backyard, a field next door,
a fence line, anywhere, I'm off for a while to smoke a cigarette, be alone, I am hiding
from other people, I am hiding from myself, I am hiding from the current story
I am living in. Sometimes it feels so good to be alone it seems we were meant to be
like that forever. Sometimes it feels so good to be with another person its seems
we were meant to stay with them forever. Forever and ever. The words that cannot last,
but try to. They carry more heartache in them than anyone can sense. They haunt us,
because they represent what we are not, they represent the absence of death, and death
surrounds us, forever does not surround us but it finds us, in moments, in minutes,
in the breeze. So blow, and blow, and blow. Blow slightly. Blow lightly. Bow before
a power greater than thee. And the fence goes from here until the darkness. It goes on.
With the cattle on one side and the goats on another side and the children on both
sides with their hands out, a bit of feed there, hoping to gain a small amount of trust.
You can either see truth in an animals eyes or you can mistake what you see of yourself
there as truth. Or nothing. Or everything. On a river in Missouri there is a small, stone
prison, only feet from the water, and indeed if the water gets high the prisoner gets wet.
But this is an old prison, it is history now and holds no prisoners, only young kids
and curious adults who climb out to take a look. Bars looking out to the quick, moving
water, and I think I could have once committed a crime in this county. So people jump off
the top, and do flips off the top, and swing around the stone walls. And I stare
at this prison that has become a piece of amusement equipment, and wonder who
stayed here, how long they stayed here, if their feet got wet at night, if their feet
stayed wet at night, and cold, and dark. Not too far away I watch a snake slide out
and into the water. Perhaps it is a symbol of a soul set free. Perhaps it is a symbol
of evil returning. Perhaps there is no such thing as a symbol, perhaps symbols are just
another form of terror that humans have supplied to the natural world. As a child,
the argument they made was this: God made man and man made this and therefore
whatever man makes is also made by god. But it is also: Man made god and man made this
and man will continue to make whatever he wants. These are not of the summer,
necessarily. These are not dictated by the summer breeze. But rather in contrast to.
The difference of what the water returns, of what floats and what does not float. Of what
hovers just under the water. And the sweat drips there, and the water carries it
away, to more water, more water, more water. A drop in the ocean. A single grain
of sand. Dust in the wind, and doesn't rock and roll say it right sometimes. And say it
so, and say it sentimental, and say it because it had to be said. We've got a little boom
box next to the shore, or else in the water itself, we are sitting inside inner-tubes,
tipping them back and listening to the local classic rock station as it makes its way
through the ash, the cypress, the cedar. On a day like today you could believe
the world began once, that it was new once, first loved once, first lost once, first

everything. Do we return, or will we return, or can we return, or do we even want
to return. Why, yes. Why, no. I wouldn't change a thing I'd change everything.
And one thing leads to the next thing, one glance to one conversation, one conversation
to one kiss, one kiss to one sleepless night on a couch with some old film on
the television, some old film about love, or the separation between the sexes,
or harmony, or they're singing some songs and getting fuzzy on the edges. We're all
a little fuzzy on the edges, a little blurry, a little warped, you know—look close enough
and you will see that your arm doesn't end where the air around it begins, nothing ends,
nothing begins, but it's still sometimes easy to believe it's so, or it's still sometimes easy
to believe it's not so, it's easy to believe anything sometimes, and this is frightful,
or fearful, this is why we put a flag into the earth, a foot on the mound, a hand over
a heart and make pledges and vows and commitments against the great unknowns.
We're shape-shifters, all of us. We are all chiseled out in stone. Nature and nurture,
last night there was a show on about a famous actor, gone to cocaine, and then crack,
and then rehab and out and rehab again. He said he couldn't help it, his disease, his
biology, and we are all biologies, we are all textbooks, with green leaves on the covers
and the euphemistic anatomy of the human bodies inside. The human bodies.
In the summer, in dresses, in boots, in bathing suits. We're all sweating just enough
to almost glimmer. We do glimmer. The train whistles at everything so beautiful, so right,
so endangered at the crossing. I take the Johnson grass and place it between my fingers,
and stretch it taut, and blow, and whistle back. I whistle with the formation of my mouth.
I whistle with a candy wrapper. I've learned to make noise, and it is good to make noise,
I whistle and the dog comes running, a little blood on the tooth, panting, cocking his head
at the noise, the refrain of the whistle, as the kettle whistles, too, and the train,
and the heat of the summer whistles and a man whistles and a woman whistles
and a chorus of whistling begins to take over the world. And it rises, and disturbs
another on a porch somewhere who whittles, who wants only quiet, or else only
the bird's whistle, which is a song not a whistle, but together we can make them
the same thing. So he takes a block of wood and a pocketknife and shaves the bark.
Then shaves the knots. Then shaves the shape of a face, a mouth opening, a mouth
trapped trying to say something from its home deep in a cut limb, a dead limb,
an old limb, a limb of a hard consistency. And back on earth they were getting along
for one day—at the public pool, flips off the diving board, children and adults
in line for the slide, a day of recreation and cooling off, a day of splashing
and reading and books just dying to get a little wet, too. And everywhere the world
goes on. In the trash can, the maggots. In the port-o-potty, a black widow
with a nest under the seat to catch the flies. They are all so clever, the creatures
that crawl, the spider that comes up the drain, and up the drain, and up the water
spout. So Charlotte spun a web and I am spinning a web. Spinning a tale of summer,
of summer woes, summer love, a great tale of human compassion and shortcomings.
On the Rio Grande, a group of wild boars swim across the river, not knowing
they are leaving one country and entering another, not knowing the ease with which
they are passing through. And the wind comes across freely, too, and the summer
breeze, and the birds, but not the humans, for we are something else, or we have
fashioned ourselves as something else, sitting in cantinas on either side, our shirts

drenched, our feet tired, a good bottle of beer turning in our hand. Make it a double, bartender. Make it one for the end of the world. Make it one to put hair on my chest, to help me forget about the past, put a quarter in the juke, play a song on the box, play another, and one just for me, and make it sad, or else nothing sad. So the box lights up and a record spins, and two people spin each other across the dance floor, and others lick the salt, take the tequila down, and bite deep down into a slice of lime. The summer honky-tonk, the summer fiesta, the summer we had nothing better to do so we went out, sometimes, we danced, sometimes, we drank cocktails and beer and escaped to the parking lot to smoke a joint, and look up at the stars, and bring the stars down to us, closer to us, as one with us there, beside the pick-ups and econo-models, the crickets and the bottles busted in the gravel. If this is one place, one bar, one booth, then it is everywhere. And if it is everywhere then you are here. And you are here, and I am here, and we are here together. We are singing together, smoking together, drinking together, or doing nothing together, staring at each other together, folding napkins together, burning matches together, turning a sugar packet over and over together, wanting just to rip into something sweet, searching for the courage to do so. Salt, pepper, ketchup, hot sauce, steak sauce. Additions to the table-top ambience. The hunger continues. The hunger persists. The hunger walks inside, from the throat down to the gut, and the gut speaks, the gut as American prophet, Cassandra gone down to Cassie, Cassie to Cass, the gut that says something other than the brain, an alternate discourse, another text, another message, another form of logic altogether, or not logic at all, the opposite of logic, the gut as that which grows over time in each man and each woman, because it has not been let out, it has been silenced, or passed over, and so each day it expands a little bit more. So we fill it with food, and place our hands on it after dinner, and shake it, and talk to it, but still it grumbles and moans. But what does it say? And what would your people do with you if you listened? How would you explain yourself? There is no explaining, no way to explain, only the impulse, the chill, the electricity, the pull. And the pull, pull, pull. As the waves pull. As the cliff's edge pulls. As the water in places pulls, and pulls you down, and down until you are pulled away from the difference between being pulled and not pulled, from knowing difference at all. Between sickness and wellness. Good health and bad health. West Nile and a bad summer fever, or else just fever from the heat—from too much sun, too much time, too much of serving too many people. And we all serve someone, just as Dylan said. And Dylan has said a thousand things, and a thousand things worth repeating. This is his song. This is your song. This is not a song at all but a poem trying to be a song, words trying to be a song, people trying to be songs, music trying to break you down somewhere inside, down deep where you feel the earth resonate, resonate and twang like the rusted cone on an old dobro, steel on steel, slide, blues, blue. We've all got the blues. And a little make you moan. And a little more make you groan. Let it out, now. Let it go. Holler, and I will holler with you. Holler to the depths of the blue water, the green water, the black water that goes deep as you want it to, deep as you imagine your holler can reach, to the catfish down low, the darkness down low, on beyond to the icy depths of hell. Hell,

Hello, are you still down there in our recollections? I remember. I remember everything, some things I'd hoped to forget, but my mind will not forget. Some things I hope never to forget, this summer I hope never to forget, it is a vow of memory I make, it is hope for the future, the long, long road ahead—middle age and old age and age beyond any conception of age, just being tired as the earth is tired. I live another day. Beyond this I have no control, and of this I have no control. It was dying in a dream, my own death dramatized, and I was that dramatized narrator, at once an other and at once myself, dying so quickly, so smoothly, so painlessly everything turned black and quiet, like going under water, just for a moment, to escape the heat, but once there finding reason to stay, reason to hang on to a rock down below, reason to sit cross-legged on the floor of the river while the water pulls you onward, and your buoyancy pulls you upward, reason to fight that pull, reason to let reason go, to let the air in your lungs go, and sit, quietly, with nothing, and no thoughts, only the sensation of water coming across you, and under you, over you and around you, a baptism without words, or procedure, a baptism let loose of etymologies, histories, religions, and the whole wide world. And then you come up, you rise to the surface, and the sun is there again, and perhaps your friends are there again, and the radio is still playing rock and roll and people are still swimming and screaming and laughing and the same, they are all the same but they are not the same, either, because you are not the same, I am not the same, we have been under and seen the water as it runs against water, the variations between the current and stagnant pools, we have been to the river, we have been dipped in the water, we have been washed. But to anyone else it may not matter. Or, perhaps to a girl sitting in a suit on the side, looking out, watching the people, watching you, as you went under, and she was holding her breath, too, for a little while, she was holding it for you, who had gone under, for herself, who had watched another go under, and so you were both under there, and I was under there, and we were a family that stays under there for a short while, for as long as we can, before the lack of air brings us back. And life brings us back, the living brings us back, and as we come out of the water with a gasp, she lets out her own gasp, and stares a bit longer, then lays down on her back and looks up through her sunglasses to the sky, the clouds moving slowly, the sun in and out of the clouds, and then she becomes a cloud and for a brief moment is altogether gone. Gone fishing, the sign on the door read. Gone for a walk. Be back soon, or else, I'll never see you again. But I will see you in your dreams, and you will meet me in mine. I will see you in the summer, when everyone is going away, on vacation, to the beach, across the ocean, I will see you when your clothes are wet. Another porch, and the crack of a beer can. This is the refrain. Or one refrain, there are many. The buzz of the mosquito. The sound of a foot kicking water. Fish in the fryer, meat sizzling on the grill. An ice-cream maker turning and turning in the background, the machine resonating, the cone resonating, waiting, and I am talking to someone far across a table, we are in our own conversation and there are other conversations, there are a thousand conversations to step into, to step out of—there is local gossip and talk of the climate and the president and evil men, or a debate about evil men, what is evil, evil societies, since the good is assumed to be inherent in the speaker. And on and on, and the hum of the machine goes on,

and we forget about it until the ice-cream maker kicks off, the silence so loud
it quiets us, too, a click, and then nothing, and then dessert is ready. Silence can be
the loudest thing in the world. Like Oklahoma thunder. It's what wakes us
in the night when the power goes down. Not the thunder, or the lightning's strike,
but the loss of electricity, the hum of the household machines, the a/c, everything
kicking off at once and the silence coming down like a brick on the floor, while I jump
from the sheets and look out across the house, waiting for some ghost to come
and swoop me away. Never-ending silence, nevermore. The raven come down
for me with a piece of white gown in its beak. So I sit up, I sit up with the darkness,
the summer storm, the wind, the thunder and lightning. Once during a heat-lightning
storm, I saw a tree struck, and unlike most trees it was not split in half, it was not torn
apart but took the lightning as a piece of dry wood takes the flame, and it was on fire,
from top to bottom, red coals covering every branch. And seeing this in the darkness,
seeing this tree lit on a road that no one else was on, only my cousin and me, it was like
seeing a prophecy in action, seeing the burning bush, seeing a message though
I have no idea what that message was. It said Believe in me. It said Believe in yourself.
It said Believe in whatever the fire tells you to believe in, and burn, burn, burn. And I say it
to all of you: burn. I say it to myself: burn. Burn for another and burn for yourself
and burn for love and loss and burn to be free and burn to run and burn to go and burn
to stay and burn in the sun and burn from the summer heat and burn with your hand
next to a campfire and burn the marshmallows on that fire and burn in your tent at night
and burn the next day again in the sun and burn for it all and burn, burn, burn. I have things
I would show you if I could. You have things you would show me. We have stories
we would tell each other and one day we will become the story together. The river runs.
The rain comes and the water rises. The crops drown. Even several people in Texas
drown. And the rain leaves and the sun comes and the crops spring back to life.
It's a circle. It's not symmetrical at all. It's a circle not as geometry but as mythology—
a circle that really has nothing to do with a circle. It's more up and down, back and forth.
It's me in the back seat of a suburban, riding on some summer vacation with an
etch-a-sketch, trying to draw the billboard of a local restaurant. And the lines moving
and my fingers moving but nothing working—only scribbles and patches, straight lines
and crooked lines. Summer is for the crooked. The crooked barn getting the new tin roof.
The crooked men drinking coffee and talking crooked shit about the other people
they call crooks. The crooked walking stick I pick up beside the lake, and walk with,
feeling like walking, feeling like I could use some help. Tell anyone about this, and I'll come
back here and kill you, and your family, and your horse, and your dog, and even the ants
that crawl around your sugar bowl, and I'll burn your barn and house to the ground.
A crooked thing to say, but I was crooked that day. And a plane comes down again,
not a crop duster but a small passenger plane, and the pilot takes a practice landing
and then heads back up into the sky. The summertime air show. Once I was driving
down the interstate and out of nowhere an old bomber was flying right toward me,
blowing up the field next to the road, and this was not long after the 11th, so I thought
I was under attack, I thought to myself I never thought that it would happen
like this. And it was happening. The plane was coming and the field was getting blasted
into a thousand pieces. But the plane let up and the bombs died down and it turned out

23

to be just a production for an air show. But the productions are so real sometimes,
or can seem that way. Tonight we present the tragedy of summer, with life played
by the sun, and death played by the sun, and both also played at times by the rain. The snake
will be played by the snake. And summer is the season of the snake, or of the summer snake.
At the water's edge, it swims up and stares for a moment, it swims right between the legs
of your chair in the water, it swims where it wants, being a snake. So some boys will leave
them alone. Some boys will go out and catch them, and scare their friends or mothers
or friends of their mothers. Some girls will do the same but because of this
will be called tom-boys. So you see it was Adam who thought that he gave the names,
but it was the snake that made them, being the dividing line, things being either
of the snake or not of the snake, for the snake or against the snake, and the names
just kept lining up. But a plea for the snake. The snake knows nothing of good and evil.
Or else the snake is both good and evil and knows all about it. We are all all about it.
Read all about it. It can be found in any book since the beginning of books. So a snake
swims next to me, and I watch him and he watches me, or she watches me, I have
no idea how to tell the sex of snakes, and care not to look that close anyway.
And care little for sexes, anyway—I just stare at the snake with its head on top
of the water, and others swim away, but I stay, and the snake stays, and then we each
say Thank you for the time because we've got manners today, we say this and we go
our separate ways. So, more breeze, and gas grills for sale. Discount today. Discount
tomorrow. Discount the thousand things I have told you. And at the Dollar Store people
are in love. At the Wal-Mart people are in love. At the IGA people are in love. And people
are buying detergent, cheap boxes of soap, smelling cantaloupes, squeezing tomatoes,
even mourning a bit that the tomatoes are at last so good, and ripe, and round and wet.
It can't stay this way. They'll be gone in October. So everyone who has a little patch
of yard puts them out, or on the porch in a small planter, and the tomatoes come
in the summer, they fill the gardens, and their sticky stems and leaves shoot up, and out,
against the cage, rattling the cage, tied to a stake through the middle of their heart.
The tomato is the summer heart. People growing tomatoes are the summer heart.
So, eat your heart out. Sing your heart out. Let your heart out to grow wild with the weeds,
to come on with the heat, and the water, and the weather. And walk through the rows,
the itch of the leaves on your arms, the small bugs crawling underneath those leaves,
and the smell not of tomatoes but of the plants that produce tomatoes, a smell
of sunshine and dirt and summer. Use your senses. Open your eyes. Look out the window
and let your mind wander through the garden. The garden is open. The garden is free
of charge. Bring me back a watermelon. Bring me back a squash. The season of colors,
and colors changing colors. Green going to brown. Brown back to green. Red and yellow
and white and purple holding ground against the turning of the grass. So the grass turns
over and sleeps. And I turn over and sleep, and there is a ghost again in the other room.
It wants nothing, I think. Only to watch me sleep, and I pull the white sheets up against
my chin. It is not cold but I am hiding from myself. And the heat comes on so no one
sleeps much these days. They walk out and check the thermometer just outside the back
door, and watch the news, with the numbers, each number corresponding to a place
they call or once called home, each temperature agreeing or disagreeing with their own
readings. And down a gravel road in a purple house a gypsy will read your palm. But you

must believe in palms. You must believe in gypsies. You must burn matches and say small oaths, or prayers, or make promises with the beginning of what burns and what goes out. So you see the gypsy. You see the crystal ball. And I watch as her long fingernails swirl a clear vision into a muddled vision, a muddle vision into a future, an array of futures, a life and a death and a duration. And your palm is the duration. And she holds my wrist like a cuff. And with her fingernails traces the duration, finding at one point either a pause or an end, she says, sometimes it is difficult to say which. So I will pause or I will end. I will intermission or else finale. And the seasons will do the same. The seasons will do to me as I am to be done to. They will take me in a cycle. They will take me up and down. They will put white hairs on my chest, lines on my face, the scars of summer work on my hands. Hands in hands. Lines in hands. The body tells a story that cannot lie. And I cannot make it lie. Not next to you. I can perceive you from a great distance, I can abstract you, abracadabra you, and Poof!, the gypsy is gone. But it is close, now. Or when it is close it is too close, unbearable, and I know that you, too, have a palm. And a pause, and an end, and a story. But is the story written? Are we writing it? Are we writing it well? I can't stand to put up with any more bad fiction. This is not fiction, it's reality. This is not reality but what we have described as real. Too real to be reality. Too real to be fiction. Too real to be anything other than something we have no words for. And need no words for, words being a kind of limitation, words being something that sometimes chains us to the ground. And they set us free, too. They do all of these things. They do what the summer does when it is at its summer best. The power lines run east and west. The power lines run north and south. The power runs through our homes, and out of our homes, and to a little generator in the woods somewhere, running a small refrigerator and the evening news. In the woods, a blue light. In the woods a spider's web. And a long chain of spiders' webs. One after the other down the dark and trodden path. Tree spiders. Great brown spiders with large thoraxes, spiky legs, weaving a tale of the darkness and the trees, slowing down what's coming by at night. Nighttime. The stars. The moon and the face of the moon. It sits there, glowing there, smirking there as if it were made for that purpose. Knowing distance, knowing that we are here on earth, and it, he or she, is up and away, free from the confinement, free from the strain, free from looking up at itself and wondering why, and how, and am I really such a small, small thing. We're all small. We're the little things that get squashed. And we are giant. And giants. And everything at once. We are baseball on the television. Wiffleball in the backyard. We are hot dogs. Hamburgers. Quarter pound, half-pound, pound. They are grinding the meat this summer. The are grinding it up and we are buying it. We are buying into the dream. We are making the dream, the American dream, we are the dream itself. And so we live the dream, or try to live the dream, or else despise the dream for what America has made of the dream, or not America but what we have made of the dream, it's not a dream anymore, it's an impossibility anymore, or a possibility depending on how we feel about the dream, and we look each morning at the dream, in the papers at the dream, in the bathroom mirrors at the dream, on the scales at the dream and in our wallets at the dream and in the trunks of our cars at the dream and our briefcases at the dream and the dream becomes too many things, and everything, it becomes the big dream to define the little dreams we have at night, the dying dreams, the flying dreams, the dreams

of women, the dreams of high school, the dreams of our fathers and mothers and falling,
walking up the stairs at an impossible rate, wanting only to get to the top, never getting
to the top, and when we wake up we are sweating and it is summer still. And summer
is part of the dream. And it is a pause in the dream. It is a momentary break, when we
go out to the water, and sit on pontoons in the water, and ski behind boats in the water,
and throw rocks in the water, and hit rocks with ball bats across and over the water,
and skip rocks over the surface of the water, so that the rocks can walk on the water,
so that the rock and the water achieve a moment of harmony, one-time, two-times,
seven, eight, nine-times, this is a competition between friends and family for another
death-defying act of the arm and physics. But physics cannot always be explained.
There is no absolute equation for the way the stone travels across the surface, because
the air is unknown, the rate of the water at each exact second in each exact spot
is unknown, the exact surface of the rock is unknown, and so it's what we get to know,
knowing that we don't know, it's how we pick through the thousands, to find something
flat, something the right size, not too light or too heavy, not too thin or too thick,
something to send out to break up the glimmer of the sun on top, something to bounce
as long as it can and then go under. And back to the darkness. And the other rocks
in the darkness. And the memory of being in that darkness, of holding on underneath,
of holding out against coming up as the rock is coming down, and passing each other
on your way. The way is long and winding. The way is gravel. The way is sand.
The way passes by a campsite, and a little bar, and a group of pine trees. The way
is to the left of the fork, the right of the fork, the east of the lake, the north of the river.
The way is here and we are here, and we are waiting for you. And I have a cold drink
waiting for you, if you can find your way, if you can bring the way to me I have
many things for you, to give to you, so I'll begin by giving you directions for how
to get here. And directions in the front seat, opened for me to look at, to guide me
to you, so that we can meet together, and share a little time together, in the summer
together, and then the summer will go its separate way and you will go your separate
way, and I will sit here for a little while and remember, and then go my way.
Shades on, visors down. The road goes on and on and on. And the cattle stand
chest-deep together in the water. It is too hot to lie down. It is too hot to get out.
It is too hot to do anything but hope, and wait, and wonder, and turn over from one
side to the other, so as to burn evenly, in the times of being out of the water.
The cattle bawl, the cattle are too tired to bawl. They are not lying down, there is no
thunder. There is a science to watching cattle. There is a system to watching cattle.
There is nothing to watching cattle but to do it, and do it patiently, and believe
that things are out of your control. Because they are out of your control. It is all out
of your control. Believe that, never forget that, forget that, take control, or else,
just let everything go. So the cattle go by, and the oil pumps go by, and the alfalfa
and fescue go by, and the barns, the houses, the gas stations, the ponds,
and at some point on I-44 I drive underneath The World's Largest McDonalds,
where they have a mini-museum for Will Rogers, and above me people are eating
cheeseburgers and French fries, eating ice cream, and looking out, looking down
at the cars coming on and going under, gone on into another dream of moving.
The reality of moving. A moving sale. Moving on. Summertime and a cool Saturday

morning, yard sales, old tennis shoes and cassette tapes, the days of cassette tapes,
be kind, rewind, rewound into an older version of the summer story, an older
version of music, an eighties version, a plastic version, a version you could reach
into and pull out the physical evidence of the sound, the narrative of the sound,
the movement of the sound from one sound to another, one wail to one whine,
one solo to another solo, and harmony, and music, and everything. In the bedroom
window there is a wasps nest, trapped between the inside pane and storm window,
and the wasps go round and round and I put my hand against the glass, and tap
the glass, and break through the glass to where the wasps stay, where the wasps no longer
stay, now they circle the air, and circle me, and circle the light in the room, and go
back to the window, wanting back inside the window, crawling against what they can
see through, see to, crawling to get back in but they will never get back in—you can't
go back, so go on, or go home, or get lost. A hot morning and a football camp
practicing in Blytheville, AR, a terrible place, a wonderful place, a place that opens
its face to the bright sun, and spreads out, flat, all across the earth. Pumping gas
and sweating, and the blur of heat in the distance, and the blur of gasoline
beside my hand, and we are blurring, we are the blur, the streak of a hand on the glass.
Stopping here, stopping there, stopping in Claremore, OK, to fill up, this time near
the home of Will Rogers, who had a thousand things to say, and good things,
and true things, and concise things. This is not a concise thing. This is a long thing,
a longish thing, a thing getting longer by the minute. Then the policeman drives by,
and the hearse drives by, and the people drive by, and we stop and watch. We pause,
and the a/c pauses, too, it slows, and we sweat, and the long parade continues
through the streets and the stop lights, to a spot in the ground somewhere.
And everything stops. Even the stop lights—stopping stops, for one long moment,
one hot moment, one moment in July before it goes on again, a bend in time,
a fracture of light and a small prism of color on the bedroom wall. A crystal, and then
another crystal, and the light stretches little rainbows across the room. And in the puddle
of gas, a rainbow. And in the diesel, a rainbow. And just after the storm, coming through
the gray, a rainbow, held mid-sky, not touching down, no gold, no gold, no gold
for the greedy people. Only beauty. And, ahh, beauty. And oooh, and ohhhh, the fireworks
show. The horses hide from the pop. The horses get hot in the pasture. And lather up,
and get foamy and white at their flanks, and thirsty, and dip their nose deep into the trough.
And we climb in the trough, too. It's too hot not to. It feels too good not to. So we are
swimming and the horses are drinking and splashing. We are in the water, and under
water, and the ground is dry and the sandburs spread out and go wild, and sticky,
and sharp, and mean. What do I mean? What do we as a people mean? What does
the summer mean on its own terms, and not in relation to the winter, the fall,
the spring. Down the road a few men sit in their driveway and take long hits
off a crack pipe. And in another room a woman sits with beads and says a prayer.
And elsewhere someone is dying right now. Someone is drowning right now. Someone
is swimming out in an attempt to get across, but not getting across. Or else getting across,
but to another place, not the shore they had envisioned, not the rocks and soft mud
they had envisioned, more than they could ever envision, nothing to envision, the vision
itself bending slowly through the room. And the vision will find you in the darkness.

The vision will find you when you wake. The vision is constant, it is fleeting, it is
everything we can't discuss. Or don't know how to. Or are fearful to. Fear, as it lives in you,
do you feel it as it walks beside you, your shadow on one side, your fears on the other,
or else the fear is the shadow itself, that which hides from the sun and in hiding fills
up its own space, turns into its own thing, exists as the light on the wall exists, becomes.
How to get away. How to go on without thinking about going on. People leave work
early and go fishing. This happens all over the world. And they pause a few minutes inside
the cool air of the bait shop, the minnows, the crickets, the worms packed in dirt
inside Styrofoam containers, a habitat of worms, a colony of worms, worms stacked on
worms in rows in glass-door refrigerators. Or else, a vending machine somewhere.
A vending machine with crickets and minnows and worms and catfish bait. A dollar in,
a box out. A step to the side and you can buy a cold soda, a bag of chips, a snack for later
in the day. The world is so convenient. And so strange, being so convenient,
and terrifying, too. We are terrified. We are so, so scared. Of dying, of living, of being
humans in the age of reason. It continues. It is beyond our control. So drink up, friends,
while the summer lasts. It will not last. There is no gold under the rainbow, or nothing
gold can stay, if there is. But I don't know. I can't make myself know and I don't know
if I want to know, or what I want to know, or how I want this knowledge to come.
The divine, it comes down on me like rain in the summer some days, and the rain comes
down on me, and the birds fly beside me, they cross my face, the birds dip in the puddles
from the rain that has come down on me, around me, surrounding me, where the expanse
of my body spreads out and keeps some things dry. And keeps little dry, comparatively.
And keeps everything dry, comparatively. The acreage of the ants, the small spiders,
crawling across the Bermuda grass, through the web of the little things, the life of the little
things, spreading out, searching for food, bringing food back, the call and another
refrain, the ants marching, the spiders jumping, the mosquitoes buzzing everywhere
on the surface. And they fill that surface up. They are the holy groundskeepers of the ankles.
They are expanding, they are taking over the world, they are the summer itself
set to flight and set to remind us of the summer itself, the goodness of summer, the itch
of summer, the pull to get in a car and just take off. And they are in the car, too, so I roll
the windows down, and turn the a/c on full-blast, and the air blows, and the mosquitoes
come from below and go out through the windows, from the cool air to the hot air,
from a cool breeze to a summer breeze, and I am at one with all of it, the inside
and the outside, the car moving and the ground staying still, the difference telling the story,
telling a story that is the same story, another story, an alternate story, of existence.
The summer will not end today, but it will end, nonetheless. And it will return, nonetheless.
After I am gone. After you are gone. After we have returned to the same spot and looked
each other in the eyes, our eyes saying it was a good day, it was a summer day, and nothing
more, nothing less, it was hot and we sweated and when touched our skin slightly stuck,
and in that moment we, too, stuck, even after we left, after you went one way and I went
another—it is here now, it is gone now, it is everywhere and blowing across the sky now.
It is forever now, so drink from the cup when you're thirsty. It is forever and forever
will be gone before you know it, it will return before you know it, it will splash water on you
or sweat you out, it will heat you up, burn and burn you, it will forever remember your face,
and the breeze on your face, and the bright sun as for a moment it filled you, and you shone.

And of passing and everlasting beauty I have nothing more to say, I have everything more
to say but not the means to say it. I will go to the window. I will remember you there.
And remember me as one standing against the glass, a forehead pressed against the warmth,
a hand breaking through the glass, the heat and the blood and the noise of the world
outside filling the room, everything together in the room, everything humming as the summer
hums at night, as the a/c hums, as the cicadas hum and wheeze and scream, the noises
running together, filling the vacuum of noise, filling everything so that it becomes
a silence, but its own form of a silence, a summer silence that is a resilience against silence,
a long tune at dusk and on and on through the night. And outside the window, outside
the back door a cicada leaves its shell, and it is new, and bright green, and born again,
in the heat we are all born again, and tomorrow the insect will be something else,
a handsome male, taking air into its abdomen and rattling it like a small drum through its
timbales, the death rattle, life rattle, come hither sweetheart rattle, the mating call, changing
to the courtship call, a quieter call, a purr almost, and in the trees they purr together,
and rattle together, and echo each other, and fill the limbs and the leaves so as to scare
off the birds, hide from the wasps that would eat them, give volume to the tree as a means
to replenish what they take, to refill what they remove from the deciduous landscape.
And it is love between the cicadas, or just mating. It is not being able to recognize
the difference. It is everything. And in the tall grass the female cardinals bicker with
the other female cardinals, and the male cardinals bicker with the other male cardinals,
and they also bicker with each other, being red, scarlet, shades of each under
the soft brown of her wings, and above the soft gray of his. The birds watch the bugs,
constantly, and the fat black cat in the field watches the birds, constantly, and I watch it all.
On the news there was a story of a cat in a nursing home, a cat indifferent to humans,
as many cats can be, but occasionally this cat would crawl into bed with someone,
roll in a ball next to them, and purr, and stay there all night. And each time within a few
days, that person would die, and so the others noticed the cat was calling out death's
name in its purr, it was pointing fingers, saying This one, too, shall pass. And the doctors
were giving reasons, science, but this is not about science, it is about an animal
that hears something else in the heart, and the blood, that smells something else, knows
something more than the rest of the cats that crawl through people's legs all day,
and ask to be petted, for a little rub on the back. And August approaches. August sighs
against the back of my neck. It is coming, and signaling the end of what is coming,
and the beginning of something else. We are in the dog days now, boys and girls.
We are letting our tongues hang out. And low, and to the left, like some thoroughbred
out-panting the others at the end of July, a winning ticket, the winner's circle, and air
drawn in to its hot mouth, where the bit is pulled taut, where the lips barely begin to foam
around the edge. The bit, the reins, the leather. A long summer's ride through grasslands.
A campfire, the hub of an old semi wheel over the fire, as a little oven, and we cook
barbeque and beans and drink bourbon at night and tell tales of the summers gone.
And still the cicadas. Always the cicadas, always so that they fade into silence, as their
constancy leads us to forget, or forget for a little while, until we hear something in
the distance, and listen, concentrate, while the sound grows louder and louder,
and the rattle, and the hum, and the ebb and flow of one tree to the next, they are
the summer breeze in the form of music, chorus, constancy, song, sound surrendered

to biology. Then in the distance a lawnmower starts, and each passing of the motor mocks
the cicadas, or pays homage to them, the thick grass cut down to its roots, to where
it once began, where it will begin again, and go on, and on, until the fall takes it over.
So stay. Just a little bit longer. It has been a long day and the sun has worn me out, I am
hungry, thirsty, I am waiting for your permission to begin. So the dog days, and in
an asphalt parking lot near the edge of town there is a small wooden shack selling
sno-cones, of all flavors, the colors of the rainbow put to syrup, put to names:
Tiger's Blood and Wild Raspberry and Jamaica. Jamaican me crazy, mon.
And the heat can do it to anyone, as it becomes too hot to fish, too hot to tend
to the garden, too hot to do much of anything but sit beside water, and dip yourself
in the water, and drink whatever is cold for the drinking at hand. Outside the garbage
truck beeps, and the men chatter and cough and gag at what the summer has done
to our leftovers. I sit in the attic and sweat, and go through old chests, old pictures,
old boxes of my old people, the white linen pajamas of a great, great uncle returned
after he died in a psych ward somewhere in Arkansas. A beautiful orange hat from
the thirties. I sit in the attic with the wasps who have found a way in, who always
find a way in, and build a home, and nest, and produce more wasps, and the nest
grows, additions upon additions, fifty little apartments hanging down from the ceiling
by a tight thread. Renters. And we're all renters. So I sweat and go downstairs and pour
myself a drink. And the glass sweats, and the ice cools the alcohol for a moment, and then
me, and then one drink turns into another and another turns into the evening
and the evening turns into good music on the stereo and the good music turns over
to the other side, the record spins, into the next morning and a headache under the hot
sheets. So I go out and buy my own sno-cone, and crunch on the ice as a child, and feel
the hot sun on my skin, and it is not painful but too much could be painful, it is just right,
it is warm and I am baking, I'm something sweet in the oven for you, I'm cooking now,
and the cars just keep driving by. Windows rolled down, windows rolled up, it all
depends on how well your compressor is working. A little Freon before the fall
begins. A little Freon from you local mechanic. A little Freon and the mist of the refill
coming out through the vents, the cold smell, the chemical smell, the thought
of what we sacrifice to be comfortable. And we all sacrifice so much. We give up,
we give it away. But sometimes we'll never let go. Or can't let go. Or don't want to
let go even when there's little left to hang on to. But hang on. And hold on tight.
It's a windy road and this bike gets a little bit loose above sixty-five, a little bit shaky,
a little wild, and the front tire spins itself out of control, into speed, into more speed,
into whatever comes next. So we sit on the truck bed and take turns spraying
mosquito repellant on each other, over our other scents, we mask our humanness
and cologne and perfume with something oily coming out of a green aerosol can.
I am hiding from the bug. I am hiding from my chemistry. And even with all this
the mosquitoes will not hide—they will travel, as the motorcycle traveled, across
every inch of your skin, every pore, and find the place where you have failed to remember
them, or guard yourself against them, they will suck clean your heel to the bone,
Achilles. They come and they'll come back. And the ants will come back, to my sugar
bowl, it is sweet there, and small there, and they are hungry there and taking things
back, to feed the others, to carry on the collective dream of all the ants, whatever

that be—to live, to build a home, to struggle, to claim a very small existence for oneself on the earth. And the earth goes round, it goes round and it gets dark, and then light, and then bright, and one day the moon is nothing but a sliver and the next day it is a little bit bigger, and then bigger, and then full, and then we know it. We know it right above the tree lines, as a huge, yellow, sagging face, we know it when taking the first shot of whisky at a bar that night, we know it rolling the garbage out, we know it in our hearts even before our hearts know it in our hearts, we know it as the cat knows when to purr, and who to purr next to, and how—we know it as a wild, wild pull. And it pulls us onward. And at the events arena the tractor pull. And monster trucks, perhaps the best name of all, trucks turned into beasts with enormous tires and loud motors, trucks not hiding what they are underneath, or can be underneath, bone-crushing bigfoots of the automotive race. And poor Bigfoot is sweating himself somewhere, with a salmon carcass, weeping that he has become mythology, or legend, weeping that he's so soft inside and can't tell anyone, or can't show anyone, because he is already known as a thousand things besides himself, he is known in the books, on the television, he is known as the full moon is known, and so he takes some time to try and know himself, in relation to his self that others have created, that we have created, that I create a little bit more of right now. Where does the self exist, on what plane, for what ostensible purposes, does it change, does it stay the same, is it that which looks back some mornings in the mirrors, which on other mornings we can't seem to bring into the light? A lamp turns on and the darkness pauses. The light and darkness pause together at the edge of the shadow the shade makes, the threshold, and at that place there is something stirring in the in-between—a moth or moonlight or the memory of something sinister, something holy, something held for a while then let go. So climb up the ladder, and then let go. Go up the stairs and let go, let go, let go into the wild ride of a waterslide, the water park, the wave pool as it pulls against your body, the simulation becoming motion, the motion becoming a pulse, a pulse against your pulse, the waves against your waves, and I'm sitting on the side waving, too, I'm waving at you with a drink in my hand, a towel over my shoulder, the other shoulder getting red. Walk out into the water. Go further, and deeper, and down into the many colors of the park, the slides that curve and the slides that do not curve and the slides that drop you to the ground from over one-hundred feet in the sky, you fly down with your legs together, your arms crossed over your chest, you fly down like a mummy set to motion, sent back to the underworld. People are smiling today. Remember that. People are relaxing, and forgetting about work and home and holidays and that the summer will soon be over. It is August now—it's no longer a threat but a reality, the second day of August, and down the road they're selling Indian tacos out of the side of a big white truck— fry bread and meat and beans and cheese, lettuce, tomatoes. The triumphant return of the tomato. They are huge right now, ripe right now, right, right now they are perfect. Perfection is possible but it is fleeting in its possibility. It is the life of a fly, from maggot to adult to dead in one day. The ephemeral. Welcome to the Thunderdome. And hanging from a rafter in the barn the fly tape, catching hundreds, you just put something sticky out and curiosity is enough, or glue is enough, or the sugar that has melted on the counter is enough. Enough with enough. On to something else.

The hay comes in, and we stack the hay in the loft. I am a child in this story, I am
stacking around a small opening in the back, a hidden feature, a trap door, a little
place where we will come to hide, and hide tobacco there, under the cat bed,
where the cats do not sleep, the cats are out, eating mice, these are the wild cats
that yowl as if translating death. And then it is years later, it feels like a hundred years
but it is not that long, my high school class reunion, handshakes, hellos, everyone
is staring at each other, trying not to look too hard, too long, seeing old girlfriends
and boyfriends and being surprised at what sight does, sight is a strange thing, a pang
returns, a longing returns, high school returns as a giant hologram hovering between
us all, and ten years later we occupy that space, we miss that space, we despise that
space and long to hold each other again. We don't hold each other again, but we hug
a little, we do hold a little, a little bit longer than necessary but not long enough
to mean anything. Or else meaning something, meaning everything, hoping
that it means something for all of them, too. It means little. It means a glass
with ice and whiskey, cold beer, a DJ and karaoke and a night to remember,
to embarrass ourselves, to swim later in someone's pool—we own the pools now,
we have taken the pools from the parents, we are fat and sassy and it's nice
to swim, to be able to swim and drink without the fear of a curfew or the police
or anything else, but the fear is gone, the thrill is gone, and B.B. King on the radio,
pulling at his guitar, pulling at Lucille, and lights in the pool and lights around the pool
and it's a difficult thing to grow up. So the blues, again. The Blues Hour with Elwood
naming them off one by one. We are all being named. We are naming ourselves
with the sticky nametags, we are misnaming ourselves, we are whoever we want to be,
who we were back then, who we are now, we are several versions of a blue creature.
We shine. Even in the darkness we shine because we want to, or have asked to, or else
just can't help it—we're being bright humans. Not bright in the intellectual sense
because that seems to matter less as we get older, but bright in the bright sense, that we
have taken the sun from the day and propelled its energies into the night, we have
propelled ten years ago into the night, we have propelled like the old prop of a wooden
ski boat, nostalgic and functional and almost too pretty to drive. But, drive. Drive past
the summer, drive through the summer, this is a tour, this is tourism, this is a last
chance to see, to remember, to be. Drive past the boys and the men playing basketball
at the edge of town, inside chain link, sweating, cussing, swinging elbows, and boxing
out and no one's calling fouls today. There are no fouls, and nothing foul, not even
the stench of a dead skunk on the road, so take it in, and take it on, and drive on,
past the motorcycle shop, the men and women out front in leather and denim,
the chrome, the black, the bandanas tied tight across their heads, holding the sweat
in, holding the hair in, holding some version of rebellion even though it has stopped
being rebellion, but it is rebellion today, so rebel. And the rebel yell. The holler.
Roll the windows down and let it out, and let the car out, into overdrive and on
and into something fast, something gone, something with a big motor that's been
waiting for you to say: Go. Or else just cruise through the side streets, see it all,
see it slowly, give a little music back to the grass as it fights one more time to return
despite the heat and the dry spell. No dry spells today. No rain, no ma'am, but the promise
of rain. And on television a commercial for the water park, a promise for a good time,

and a good time was had by all. The hotels and the motels, the doors open, the people
with their children in the pools there, the other people in the hot tub, it is too hot
for the hot tub but we are too fond of the heat right now not to get in. So I get in,
I get out of the car, I get out of the tub and into the sprinkler—I move through
the realities of summer, the fantasies of summer, I move through one day, and another,
but I take them one at a time, slowly, with precaution, I throw caution to the wind
and the wind takes it, and it takes it as a summer breeze, and the summer breeze
at our backs, pushing me onward a little, cooling me off a little, drying the water
on my neck so that a chill hits me, and it is a thousand things—it is death and the comfort
of dying and life and living and water evaporating seconds before a mosquito takes
its place. This is my place, right now. This is the only spot I want to be. I have been
everywhere at once but I am here now, and a man a few feet away is speaking another
language on a cell phone, a long conversation on a cell phone, but I am wanting quiet
so I make him part of the quiet, and the cicadas part of the quiet, and the thousand
longings inside me part of the quiet, and we are still together, we are not saying
a word together, we are gone into a long story of another place, of this place exactly,
a dream of the ice cream truck coming round, playing music, the electric ring
of some children's refrain, over and over, through the back streets, and my street,
he plays the song and we all come running to the song, or in our hearts we will run
to the song, and something cold, and something sweet, and something to sink
our teeth into or else move carefully around, not wanting to hit the nerve, but hitting
the nerve—and going on that nerve a long, long way. Lordy, we are sufferin'.
In the heat we are sufferin' and at the wedding reception drinking warm wine
and eating dollar roll sandwiches we are sufferin' and we are sufferin' humankind,
man, we are sufferin' the summer, woman, we are sufferin' the g that we dropped
off outside Topeka, the g with its thumb out and a duffle and an honest face.
And though the face may be honest the façade may not. Underneath we've all got
another story to tell, we've all got an itch, a rash, a summer swelter heating up
our souls or our hearts or our biological and/or chemical longings. And in the pool
they pour the chemicals, sometimes too much and so the blond hair slowly goes
green, and the girl who sits a few booths away at the lunch restaurant goes
from starlet to something out of a horror film, a swamp, a legend of long green locks.
Lock us away, we can't stop doing what we're doing. And throw away the key,
and also the man who threw away the key, there's no other way to stop it.
Fuck, he says, into the water where he dropped his watch. Fuck and fuck and fuck,
that was my favorite fucking watch. And it goes down deep, past its own recollection
of time, into timelessness, down there where we have been, and up from, below
where we have been, to the pressure where the ears pop, sound pops, and the glass
on the face of the watch holds tight and then eventually gives in. Give in
to the elements. The periodic table. Periodic because we are all periodic, of a certain
time, place, destination and departure, we are distance formulas, we are back to school
specials—new tennis shoes and new jeans and new pencils and a new backpack
to store the bloody souls in the books on which we stand. And we stand on the levee,
and the physical levee and the levee as metaphor underneath and the concrete and steel
underneath and the dirt and then the grass and then us and we are triumphant,

we are sufferin', we are wailing and hollering in the hopes of opening a hole, our voice
as a way to get back home. And out in the field the stallion is tied to a post on a long rope,
being too wild and too ready to jump out of any fence at some smell on the wind,
being too ready to hurt himself, lame himself, kill himself in an attempt to be free. Live free
or die, he says to himself each night, testing the rope in the darkness, while in a barn
not far away the bug zapper emits a pale blue light, a blue light against his black coat,
and the bugs come toward the light or else they are indifferent to the light, but it is
electric, and it is lighting up the sky. And the sky shines back, blue for blue, the moon
and the stars and a plane beeping across there. Sweet dreams, all you people.
Safe travels, and may you find what you're looking for, or get where you're going,
or simply enjoy moving between one place and another. It was hot in St. Louis and then
hot again in Memphis and when we touched down in Atlanta it was even hotter.
The summer is coming for us all, it is leaving us all, please, please, don't go, don't leave,
another moment and maybe it'll be enough. So another moment—I've got the time
if you do. And still the summer has the time for all of us. They're filling up the parking
lot at the hardware store on the weekends, they're buying more hose now, it's getting
dry now, it's not dry now but it's going to be, they're making forecasts on the television,
they're making forecasts on the internet, they're making forecasts at the hardware store
around a pick-up bed, over a grocery cart, carrying a 2x4, the summer is finally coming
on, and the rain is leaving and the heat will rise and rise and we will burn. Humankind
will burn in Oklahoma and a great fire will encompass our minds and our arms
will burn and faces will turn to the sun and burn and the wings of angels will burn
and turn to ash and the birds will sift through the rubble. If it's going to end then let it
end like this. Give us a hellish blaze, something to remember, something to take us down
with the thunder of a dry storm. Or else just keep us alive, keep us thirsty, keep us
talking and hauling bags of mulch back to our cars, bags of fertilizer, keep us cool
and upright. And in the backyard I smoke a Kool in my robe in the morning, because
it is another day and so this is my celebration of another day. I have decided to celebrate
today because why not, it seemed ripe for celebration. And the cantaloupe is ripe
and sweet and I scoop the seeds out with a spoon and get it cold, almost frozen,
so that when I am weary I can come back from the world and eat. Later that night
they made their way to the local honky-tonk just outside town, and people were dancing
there, two-stepping there, slow, slow, quick-quick, slow, slow, quick-quick, and at the bar
it was ice water for some and tequila for others and longnecks for the majority
and whiskey with sweet and sour they were having a good time it was the weekend
before it all began again it was the weekend of the rodeo and they'd been to the rodeo
and watched the barrel racers and broncs and bulls and bulldogging and ate funnel cake
and listened closely as some country singer sang songs about loss and love or else just
about the country, his hometown, about U.S.A. and damn if the people weren't beautiful.
Horse rides and pony rides in the round pin at the side for the children. Even miniature
horses for the babes. And the babes rode and the babes ate and the babes slept
and the babes cried. They cried out against the injustice of the world, the heat
of the summer, the antsy little horse under their antsy little legs—they cried out
for what they couldn't name. And along the arena fences the sponsors name themselves,
beer and tobacco companies and local insurance companies and steak houses

and churches and car lots—the never-ending advertising continues, as does the never-ending advertising of the self, of women in tight jeans and tops tied up around their torso, men in tight jeans and shirts unbuttoned, cowboy hats and cowboy boots, make-up and menthol cigarettes, perfume and cologne and belt buckles that shine. So it goes on through the night. It goes from the house to the arena to the big floor of the juke joint. And music is on the radio here, and at the club next door music is on the radio, too, and they are dancing at both places but they are dancing differently, they are strange to each other and adored by each other, they are all holding on to other people and their self-conscious images of their own bodies moving in front of other people—and so they drink and let loose and let that body go. Free them people, Pharaoh. They've got work on Monday so you'll have them back soon enough. But tonight, let them go. For the rest of the summer, let them go. They get wild and they get ornery and they get lovely and sweet. They get while the getting's good. And the cars roll down their windows and let out the music of the day, the music of the gone day, the music of one summer in 1967, or later, the music of the summer of love, played and replayed on an oldies station. Oldies but goodies. And so many summer goodies. In another month the summer will begin closing its doors, it will close down the water park, it will close down the walk-up cheeseburger joint that only opens for the season, it will close down the amusement park and it will bring the roller coaster to a halt. But right now, we are amused. And right now we are listening. We are playing our music and singing just a little bit longer. We are eating our corndogs and waiting in line. And at the end of the line wheels on steel. At the end of the line a heartbreak, a thrill, a quick ride into the darkness and back into the light, where the summer puts its show on, bright and one-hundred degrees, looking out from the top of roller coaster hill to all the world that surrounds you, looking down at the people looking up, looking in the parking lot at the people who have no idea what they're in for, or have been in it for a long, long time, and are now headed home, sun-burnt and sick from too much fried food, processed meat, sugar, the sticky fingers of the children grabbing the door handle that's hot to the touch. And the world is hot to the touch. On the street outside a dead frog flattened like a pancake, a penny on the train tracks, the face of that U.S. president stretched into a grin by heat and by pressure and because there was no where else to go but inside, into contemplation, into the air conditioning and an old recliner and a cold glass of sweet tea. Make it so the spoon stands up. Make it so it hurts my teeth. The lizards run through the tall grass and into the warmth, the grasshoppers buzz and jump and fly and eat. Walking through a tall field you can set them to music at dusk, you can wake all the world around you into flying and motion and sound without method. You are the method. And it is by that method that I come to you. Or bring you to me. Or else we find each other at exactly the same time, the right time, the time before that, the time as it propels the days forward even now, the time we halt, the time that halts us, the time that flies by like a grasshopper on the wind, Go lightly, young grasshopper, because the world it will not wait. But wait. The charcoals on the grill heat up and go from black to gray to white, and once white they are ready to burn something, anything, just give them a chance. So the meat goes on and sizzles,

and the corn goes on and cracks, and the zucchini goes on without much
of a sound, dinner will be ready at seven, come early, bring your appetites
and anything else. The checkered tablecloths on the tables outside, we're making
something out of a movie, we're writing the script as we speak, we're swinging
a clean, red and white piece of fabric into the wind, letting it air out, settle
horizontally over the space just above the table, and come down while we all
hold our breath. What a wonderful thing. It's unoriginal, it's old, it's hasn't the values
of the avant, but it is a good thing to see sometimes, nonetheless. It will not change
the world and it will not change. But the world will change, and we will change it
as we can, as we can't, as we try to eating barbequed chicken, grown men with bibs
on—he woke up out of a dream about hunger, and went to the cupboard but
the cupboard was bare. And out of the trees, the ticks fall, the ticks settle into the dark
places on the human body, the animal body, they hang on and suck the blood,
while time tick, tick, ticks away, and they get a little bigger, and bigger, and on the dog
they go gray and then purple and then blue and then at some point pop, die
and pop against the brick wall or where the dog curls around a spot on the sidewalk
and lays down. They are thirsty and we are thirsty. How many species in the universe
will drink themselves to death, or not drink at all and dry themselves to death.
The salt in the ocean as it mocks us. The sharks in the shallow water. Save your
children, save yourselves, save the greater portion of your upper thigh. They're hungry,
we've been feeding them, they're starving and you smelled so good. Survival.
Outside the coffee shop a grackle that has lost most of one foot limps after
the sparrows, and chases them away from the crumbs. Big crumbs, little crumbs,
a little bread, if you can spare it, sir, we're starved. And the sparrows feed each other,
from one mouth to another, share, share, and share alike. It is good to watch nature,
or not nature but the natural, what is natural anymore, and The Natural
with his baseball bat in the movie, sending one out of the park and making a show
of the falling lights. And the people are watching. The people are holding their breath.
And the horses are running again, saddled again, in the paddock again. And the people
are watching. And while washing their cars, while in the waiting room at the auto
mechanics, while cleaning their rims, reading newspapers, chewing gum,
while sweating over that paper and smearing the ink of one story into another,
the people are watching. And they are both stories. They are all the stories as they bleed
into one another. They are the end of the summer, they are the summer that they will
not let go. They are the cockroach with the weight of the world on its back, as it
shoulders that weight, and survives, and walks. So we walk through the heat of another
day, we walk to the same point, we meet, you and I, as rivers meet, as water meets
water, as the heat meets water and makes steam, a light fog, a hot, blurry flash of life
as it comes off the road in the distance and travels up, never straying too far
from the heat that gives it life, that burns it into blackness, redness, brightness,
that is that which will destroy you, which will resurrect you, light you, the sun as it shines
and dares you to look up, and you look up, and you see, and you are blinded.
And it is blurry. It is all blurred now—the road and what the road reaches up to,
and out to, it is a space in the distance and space meeting space. Eternity awaits.
The fall awaits. And the winter, the spring, and summer again. But this is our summer,

my summer, the summer of now and never again. So I wipe the sweat from my face
and we turn to face the light together. And we are here, and hot, and we will return
in memory and in any other way we know, and we know we will meet again, we will never
leave, we will be as the mosquitoes, and fly, and drink, we will quench the unquenchable
thirst and drink the water while it's cold, as it comes down in the rain, out through
the sprinkler, everywhere shining on the surface of everything, forever as a hot summer mist.

II. SIRE

I do not come from the blood of kings.
My name itself refers to the clay itself:
the earth that is soft when moist, solid and brittle
when fired. Compared to some I have not far to fall.
But fall we do. And when we fall, hard. Men fall.
Women fall. The world falls from its place
as cosmic center of the universe. Kings
fall—look at Lear there, sitting by the water,
wailing and moaning, the first crunch
of a brown leaf under his tired foot, the summer
turning over the green to what comes next. To leer:
to scorn, a tight snarl of the upper lip. A suggestion,
and the dog growls back. The wind blows the wild
white hair. An old man gone down to the ground,
out for the count, two left jabs, and a right hook
you never even saw coming. But the season comes,
it has begun, it has not officially begun
but Labor Day is over and done, people are packing
the ski boats up for the winter, they are parking
the campers again at the back of the house, where they
will wait for another year, where the spider will again
make her web—the jack on a block and the tires
sagging a bit at the first cold, the cold
exchanged for one last heat wave, a look
out the window, wondering if it's too late
for one more wild weekend out in the world.
A day of rest for you workers before the summer ends.
A Monday off for the laborers of the world, labor not,
love's labor not lost—gone, but not forgotten.
Soon in the mystic garden the colors will turn.
This is a recollection of the turning, the fall, the autumn
as that word hums its own tune, and whistles, and sits waiting
for a cool breeze to turn to a colder breeze, a chair
under a tree as the leaves turn and turn and crack,
a cup of coffee or bourbon resting in my hand,
something to keep me warm while reading Keats,
something to keep me going as the cicadas continue
to make their calls, their brown shells making a small museum
of the world—the physical evidence of both life and death,
change and stasis, the hard shell of a creature now fragile
to the touch. The touch, the touch, the touch.
The wind changes. The smell changes. Hold on,
hold on, and you will soon see an amazing show.

Fifty degrees, the young check-out girl says.
Fifty degrees, from a man walking out
of the local burger joint, pulling his dentures
from his shirt pocket. Fifty degrees from the weatherman, too,
and so it is true, it is coming. The number itself means
in relation to where you are standing when fifty degrees
comes. Here it is the start of something cold, or not cold
but cooler, the end of something hot, the beginning and the end,
always the alpha and omega, I am speaking now of the spirit in the sky.
And I am speaking now to that spirit. I am speaking directly
to the man/woman/beast/it who took my brother away
from me, to the ether of an idea, the reality of an idea,
to that which makes the leaves fall, which turns the landscape
from green to brown to yellow, orange, and red, while we sit
pouring piping-hot liquid from a thermos and watching.
And the turtle doves sit two-by-two on the power lines
and watch. They sit alone, and watch. They sit with feathers lost
to buckshot while flying over a field of milo, corn,
it is dove season again, and they can feel it
in their hollow bones, a howl in the wind that warns them
things will be different after Labor Day. And they will.
And they are. So the birds come to town, they come into the city
limits. They come from miles around as the people come
from miles around for the county fair. The foot-long corndogs,
lemonade made from scratch. Chicken-on-a-stick
and prize-winning hogs. And cattle and goats and chickens.
Bring your animals and they will pin a ribbon on their chests.
Ribbons of blue, red, yellow. While outside the great unknown hand
pins ribbons on nature for doing just as well—red, yellow, and orange
again. Two-thousand shades of brown. And in the fryer
the batter browns. The corn stalks browned and cut
to stubble. Then dried by enormous fans, sent to the mill, ground
down to a fine powder a small man in a little white trailer
mixes with flour and eggs and buttermilk, while outside
his temporary window the wheels go round and grind children
into a moment of delight, a moment of terror, a moment
of being outside themselves and thus children again.
Tilt-a-whirl, The Flying Bobs, The Octopus, The Zipper,
The Monkey Cages. Variations on a theme, again.
And always there must be the Ferris Wheel and the Carousel,
the lights and the sweets, one last weekend to let the excess
of the summer go, to let go, to get gone, out of the house
and away from the future, the present, the past.
So as the summer gets old it turns itself into something else.
Something comfortable being old, I am speaking to you, up there,

something in its oldness that turns into something damp.
And now the young hay bales of summer might mildew
in the pasture somewhere. And now the young summer love
might return to school. And now the schoolchildren
might grow a day older, a day wiser, one more day away
from the freedom of the day as a complete thing, a personal thing,
now given half-back to some other institution besides the self,
now coming with lunch boxes on yellow buses for an education.
And the fall is its own form of education. It is sophistication,
a pledge against sophistication, it is a leaf picked
off the ground, ground to a fine powder in your hand.
The garbage disposal takes down the last of the good tomatoes.
The last of the good corn, the last of the good peaches. Gone,
and back to their place of origin, back to the water treatment plant,
that will separate the solid from the liquid, the whole
from the void, that will clean your water and send it back
to you, with fluoride, so smile and show us all your pretty white teeth.
White against the gray sky. White against the brown trunk. A white shirt
seen from the road as a man makes an attempt to climb
a tree. Up he goes, and in he goes, and on he goes, and he gone.
Put your shoes on and get out of the house—it is nice
today, today is marked as a nice day, it is one of many
I have named, a Wednesday, a hump day, a middle day
between two other days, six other days, two seasons caught
in some limbo between the real seasons and the prescribed seasons
and the concept of seasons itself. There are no seasons. There are no
beginnings, no ends, no lines, no markers. There is the great
constant flux. There is nothing but change, change that never
changes, change that always changes, change that shakes in the pocket
of those moving around in the world, who sometimes place a hand
in the pocket, and stir the metal around to make it sing.
It is calling us. It is all calling us. It is the time
of the great white mushroom as it calls us, the time
of the teal as it whistles its song of the onset, the coming,
the prophecy of a future prophecy. It is the sound of the wind,
coming out of the north now, the monarchs swinging south first,
then soon the geese, and the ducks, then soon again we will bundle
up as that wind makes us shiver. And who asks what brings this.
And why ask, or how ask. Are you listening to me, ye who
I sometimes address, ye who I sometimes speak to, do you
hear me? What matter, and what matters. Take in the day
as it comes to you. This is a day in the long, long progression
of days. They will go on long after you and me, but we will go on, too,
as they spin themselves into the many thousand variations
of color, and love and loss and life and death and blame

and fault and hope and promise, moving on with the wind
at their backs, a new wind, the old wind, the only wind that blows
and now shakes the trees where they stand.
The trees as they stand in as barometers
for a season's soul, a sound in the void, the cicadas
still screaming and squealing. And on the pavement
the tires squeal. Rubber on asphalt, go on, gone,
here or there leaving a long black line
where something disappeared. And the thistle disappears
and goes to bloom. Bloom, and the sunflowers hang on.
Bloom, as the small purple-white asters cover the ground, and the goldenrod
reaches up. Bloom, and the boom of the leaves like fireworks,
pale fireworks of another season, subtle now, quiet now,
a spark of color against the boom, boom, boom of a shotgun in the distance.
A distance formula. A square root of the x diminished by the x,
the y diminished by the y, and the why and the where,
and the how long. A bouquet of numbers, records
in the record books, taken over once again as the whistle
blows and a kick-off is returned for over one-hundred yards,
the longest in a singular history of yards somewhere. And along the back streets
the yards go on, the Bermuda loosens its thick hold,
the sprinklers run, and today, at least, the green stays.
A small dog running in circles along the fence as I run by,
we are showing off for each other, we have no real words
to share so we share something else. I stop and talk
to an old man about weather, and his dog, a big dog,
running free through the tall grass and down to the water.
And on the t.v. every commercial is filled with NFL players
giving advice on something to buy. I buy shortening and flour,
it is the season of the pie. And as it cools off it is the season
of the chili, another strange regional concoction set to reflect
some ideological stance on beans, vegetables, meat, seasoning.
The cumin smells like an indication. The garlic and onion powders, too.
The summer chiles are now drying somewhere. It is the time
of the tobacco harvest. The turkeys once sent out to eat
the worms have become the wild turkeys edging in front
of the old Kentucky barn, where the leaves hang down
as I drive by, and on through a memory of smoke.
A match and a cigarette. A pouch of chew and an old jean pocket.
A billboard announces one last summer hurrah. Hoo-rah, and the boats
go back out on the water. Choppy water, a choppy day,
the north wind turned around and coming up from the south
against my face, from the west, coming as the heat comes
back, another week of ninety degrees, and the sweater pulled out
of the winter clothes box sits draped over a chair, lonesome and waiting

for the cold to return, the cool to return, we real cool and school
lets out every day about three-thirty. So the big yellow buses
fill the absence the big yellow buses once made. The kids
take the bikes out and ride until dark. Dark, and the darkness begins
to come earlier. And to ye in the sky, what of the light and dark?
What of the flat tire, the beer cans along the water's edge, the lure?
I am speaking now to the big fish, down deep, who in a chain
of fish eating fish holds somewhere in his body a smaller fish
with a tiny fish inside, a tiny fish with a tiny lure inside—
something sparkly and wiggly and some bright shade
of pink and green. So a man takes his shirt off and trods down
to the water's edge. He takes his line and casts it out into the lake.
The bobber floats and sends out a sort of calling, sometimes answered,
sometimes unanswered, there is always a message in the ripples
that float out from the center of the universe. But where
the center? We each become the center, and that center aware
that there must be a greater center than ourselves, or else
no center at all—it is the concept of the center itself that drives us
mad as the wind whips our hair against our faces. They'll drive the cattle,
and they'll drive the semis, and they'll drive the boats
and in the distance I make out a motorcycle being driven,
a two-stroke gassed to anger, to speed, the noise
of something dangerous held tight in another person's hands,
no longer held tight in a person's hands, let loose
over a dirt mound, to fly, to fly, to fly. And even the small wren
in its smallness knows flight. Even the big black crow going
from tree-top to tree-top. They map out a space over the water,
a space over the land, arcs going from here to there
to nowhere in particular. And I am going somewhere
particular. I am going to Memphis on a small airplane
from a larger airline sitting beside an enormous man
with enormous hands who twirls his Stetson around his fingers.
And in the airplane catalog I see they are making way for the fall.
The seasonal market. And in the airplane magazine the man
beside me points to the diagrams of the planes, asking which I think
we're on. And then he points to the flight patterns, the thousand parabolas
in a conceptual dimension marking distance and large and small planes
and large and small people and even this man I have come to enjoy
who says It's amazing more of them don't run into each other.
But we do. We have crashed together on the elbow rest
for a short while. And what does it mean to run into another?
We run into people at the grocery store, the liquor store, the concert,
the restaurants. We run into people in our lives one day and then, Boom,
our lives are not what they used to be. We have a past up to a point.
We have several separate pasts. We are the leaves that fall because

of the small weight of a bird coming down on their limbs.
We are the leaves that hold strong even against the wind or rain.
We are not really leaves at all, but we sometimes turn
a different shade, sometimes fall to the ground, sometimes crumble
in the hands of something else. And my horoscope recently told me
to listen to the language of nature, a language outside of words,
a form of communication distant and intelligent and vital
on its own terms. So I see the crow, and the turtle, and the horse,
and wonder. And in the water both the big and small fish splash,
sending out some frequency I hope to follow, but cannot exactly,
and not exactly might be the point, not exactly might be what I need
to learn, what I'm trying to learn to learn, what I can not exactly
understand or hold on to. When humans look back to their young
they tell them These are the best years of your life—enjoy them.
And so the best years become other years, but what was best,
what better, what lost and why have they given up.
What have they given up, or we, or I, or ye. It is lost
to the cold hard rain, to the thunder that seems to tear
the sky behind us, ripping the curtains, opening the mouth,
or else it is at last that mouth vocalizing something, speaking,
as I dare not command it: Speak. I ask for answers
and I get too many answers. I ask for beauty and it is too much
to hold at once. One small leaf on one small tree already gone
bright red, turned before his neighbors, his brothers
and sisters, turned early at the autumnal equinox.
The only one that read the calendar, or cared about
the calendar, or heard in the distance talk of some calendar
and just by hearing set out a map for its redness.
Sundays and football and cold cans of beer. Sundays
and long runs through the fields. Sundays and a wheelbarrow.
Some days no Sundays. Some days are easier than the others.
But do you curse the bad days for their badness? Do the days
even know themselves at all? My horoscope suggested: alternate forms of knowing.
As the turtle knows the hand on its shell, and the hand
on the turtle's shell knows the turtle knows, too.
With the rain, the fall returns. With the rain,
the summer holds on. With the rain a face looks out
the window pane, with the rain small children are getting wet,
and loving that wetness, tossing a ball back and forth in the middle
of the street, the street no longer a street but a temporary puddle,
a safe place, for a moment, before the sun comes and then the cars
come and then the children are called back into the yard.
Yesterday and the day before I was tired. Today
is a different day. What I fear most sometimes
is each of the many potential futures, each yes, each no,

each not knowing the difference. Lightning strikes, and somewhere
a small piece of the world is changed forever. Lightning strikes,
and somewhere else the power goes down.
So it is quiet now. And we, too, are quiet now.
Come now, and stand at the edge of the world.
In the distance storm sirens, practicing
for the bigger storms. Or else this is the big storm, it is
difficult to know, they have cried out Wolf so many times.
But let the wolf blow it down. And let the wolf be
blown down. The autumn steams. It is the cold rain
meeting the warm earth meeting everything that shivers
in between. Tomorrow, a sunny day. Tomorrow, a memory.
Tomorrow a quail rising out of the tall grass, the grass gone
all the way to seed now, brown and swaying in the wind.
And the wind comes in through the door without asking—
in the bingo halls, the barns, the strip clubs, the gas stations
ringing the door bell, the old man is here, making promises
through sound of his existence, her existence, the evidence of existence
supplied by a lack of existence, a push against the void, a hand
across the water, picking it up and making waves, ripples
where the sun comes down and does its thing, shining
for those who have come to see.
Everywhere the large brown tree spiders.
Closer to the water's edge the small brown frogs.
This is a late foliage rainbow, reflected on the ground.
And below the ground the root systems map out what is
above the ground, there is a system of mirrors, there is not
such a difference between heaven and hell. There is neither,
in the fall. It is the time of band practice and chili bowls.
The afternoon of the after-school special.
The early morning of hay bales and pumpkins.
And down the road there is a ranch rodeo, chuckwagon races,
a wild cow milking competition and food vendors
selling Indian tacos and cowboy nachos.
I can see the lights from here. I can hear the cows
bellowing in the chute. I can smell the horses, the sweet
dusty smell of their coat, I can feel the film it leaves
on my fingers. Arenas everywhere. And in the arenas
they recreate as competition what was once done
outside the arenas for survival, what is still done
in some places, at some times, and so on.
A slice of pumpkin pie covered in homemade whipped cream.
A cup of coffee and a cool day. The autumn is starting to fall
into place. The summer has almost completely let go.
I say this as if there is some struggle between the two,

                    and there is a struggle, and there is also no struggle
            at all, there being not two but only one constant,
this is real life and metaphor, this is the only way, the many ways,
            we can understand anything at all (if we can understand
                        anything at all). The light cuts through the window and cuts me
                            into small pieces of light and dark, little bits of the illuminated
                and the shadow. The sno-cone man is closing up shop.
        The city pool has closed up weeks ago.
The water skiers have put their water skis away for now.
            We are marking the time with what we stop doing.
                    We are marking the time with what we begin to do.
                        The season of the harvest. It's hard sometimes
                not to be thankful. The sumac berries go red,
        and then into their redness, dark and tart and boiled
with sugar for a citrus-like drink.
            Everything is going to seed, giving it back to the ground,
                    the wind, a future point of hope in something planted
                        by both method and chance.
                Comes a hawk and he makes his circle,
        and circles again, settling at the top of a telephone pole,
looking down. In the tall grass a small animal hiding.
        In the short grass a black snake slides out for one more
                day of sun, having no thoughts yet of hibernation.
                        One nation above and below the earth.
                One nation on either side of the water.
        One nation stuffing an old flannel shirt
in the front yard, making a scarecrow, not for the crows
            anymore but for the neighbors, the passersby, whoever stops
                and wants to see. He had a black hat on,
                    he had a pitchfork in his hand. He was a dark man,
                if a man can be said to be dark. Every day
        the birds quiet down a bit. The bluejay gives way
more and more to the turtle dove, the starling gives way
        to its own long shadow leading out of town, flying away
                in thousands, making an S of an exit, leaving but not
                        disappearing. And in the water the loons come
                and swim. They dip below the surface and are gone
        only to reappear elsewhere. They are time travel.
They are just having fun. They know the air and they know the water
            and right now they are still choosing to swim. It is a good day
                    to still do such things. So they yodel a bit when they let out
                        their cry. And the road construction cries out, too.
                There is much work to be done, the time to do it
        fading. Hammers on steel, bulldozers on pavement, voices
on the wind and as the humidity drops, the sound carries.

We are all carried. We are carrying ourselves—on heels,
          with good and bad posture, through the sound of leaves
                    smashing underfoot, a hum of life just below
          the surface. The band is practicing again this morning,
     they are playing a song of victory, never a tune
of defeat, they are playing a half-time special with twirlers,
     the flag girls, who take a colorful banner and bring it to life.
          You wake up, and it is October already. You wake up,
                    and November is a long way away.
          It will come in its own time. But for now October
     begins with its own story of fall, looking to Halloween, the ghosts
of another time and place, All Saints Day, the Day of the Dead
     where people mock death with bone masks in order to honor death
          for what it is, and go out to the graveyards, eat, and drink,
                    in celebration of the spirits that refuse to die.
          Come the decorations now. The pumpkins
     will soon be carved. In the trees white ghosts
hang from branches like happy dead men,
     happy to be a little sweet, a little spooky,
          a little reminder of what's to come. At the Dollar General
                    the costumes are out. There are orange trash bags
          with Jack-o-Lantern faces to fill with leaves.
     There is cautionary yellow tape for the front yard:
Enter if you dare. Soon they will dare.
     For a little something sweet they will don masks
          and sheets and fake blood on the sides of their mouths.
                    They will be hungry. It will come. The stroke of midnight.
          One Mississippi, two Mississippi. The cool weather
     is coming down, covering the brown grass
like a blanket. It is still warm in the brown grass,
     it is holding on to certain memories of the summer.
          The leaves begin to fall, slowly. Beside a small run-off ditch
                    at a park an old man in a red cap comes with his own rake,
          his own idea of exercise. All afternoon he rakes, rakes, rakes.
     This is his version of retirement. He rakes his own home,
then the neighbors' homes, then the public parks and then
     when it seems there is nothing left to rake the leaves come
          down again, they are coming down now, soon they will
                    come down like tiny sailboats falling from the sky,
          randomly, with the wind, and some will fall
     into the water and indeed sail—a crusty tip
curled against a gust, catching it, and heading out
     on a voyage with no return. And the two mallards
          will imitate. The turtles will come up to the surface
                    and watch. Was a leaf that crossed the River Styx

as if to say Death is not the end, friends—
this is one of the many lessons of the fall.
And so I have no lesson plans for classes next week.
I have no idea what to try to teach sometimes, because
it seems sometimes there is too much to teach. And I,
who myself have few answers to so many questions—
it is hard sometimes to be alive.
And sometimes so easy, so natural,
to feel the wind as something that blows, to be moved,
to be conscious of being moved and unable to explain that
consciousness, that feeling, that heart that continues to beat
in my chest. Heart and soul. How can you tell one
from the other. How does the tree favor
its limbs over its roots, or does it, or should it,
or can it. It is the time of canning now. Time to take
the last bits of the garden, pickle them, jelly them, jar them and jam them
for the cold to come. Put them on a shelf in a pantry somewhere,
put them dusty, put them old, put them away
for a rainy day, a future hunger, because if I know
anything I know I will be hungry for this moment again.
It has begun again in Martins Ferry, Ohio.
It has begun again in Stillwater, Oklahoma.
It begins again for the millionth time, which makes it
one in a million, a long shot, a small fraction,
which makes it singular and blesséd and beautiful.
At Wal-Mart they are wheeling grocery carts
full of pumpkins. There is an entire aisle of masks.
So come into the corporate light, come in and find a mask,
come in and hide, come buy, come buy,
come and represent the season.
Outside town a birthday party
and a hay ride. Young kids burrowing in that hay,
laying down in that hay, holding hands under that hay
as the crescent moon comes out and shines,
and holds us all in the hammock of its light.
Hot cocoa and spiced cider. A campfire
and s'mores. Yes, I will have some more.
Yes, there is more to be had. Yes, thank you.
Yes, moon. Yes bad music coming from your acoustic
guitar. There is better music from the acoustic world
everywhere. The owls call out more frequently.
In the dark they cross the road leading into town,
a wingspan like the dream of some shadow
that keeps passing over, keeps going, on and into
the night. We will dress as ghosts because the ghosts

50

are real in this season. As is the Angel of Death. And now
the Angel of Death is upon us, coming down on the wings
of an owl, popping up on the head of a turtle,
held in the tree spider's web—she is everywhere,
she is life, in death, the promise of life again, the fall as it foils
the spring. But take it for what it is. Take it as autumn. Take it
as wet rain making a mess of the leaves on the ground. Take them
as Keats: "thou hast thy music too."
And to the Ye that makes that music,
to the Ye to whom I assign that music,
whether it be you that make it or not, whether you be
there at all, to the Ye I sometimes pray to, sometimes curse to,
sometimes sing back to, Good morning to ye, and yea,
thank you for the cool, I am chilled to the bone by the early cold
but I can therefore feel myself to the bone,
and the heart as it slows, and beats, beats,
against the rain where it falls and drips on the porch.
Soon the cornucopia will be upon us. Soon the harvest,
soon gourds, soon tableside. It is all one constant cornucopia.
It is all that which fills you up, which empties you,
it is that cold white hand holding the gas nozzle
at the pump, the steam of some stranger's coffee.
And stranger, you are welcome to it.
We drive off and we sometimes pass the small
wooden bridge, while the weight that we carry
on our shoulders presses down, and the tires sag,
and the bridge sags, and all the world sags
for a moment, and creaks as something old,
something wet, something calling out asking only to be heard.
The wet tarp blowing on a bail of cotton.
The wind comes. Hail comes and hell comes.
The wind pushes through, and takes the tarp away,
takes the cotton away—cotton in the streets,
cotton on the highway, an early snow,
a dirty white picking up and blowing its seeds
away. Hot soup and a big spoon. Coffee at the cafe.
This is the open road. We are the haunts. We are spooky.
We move and we shake. Shake the leaves off the trees.
And then the big horse with the bad eye gets spooked, too.
Go in. Go into. Put the storm windows up,
lock the doors. The Byrds on vinyl singing Turn, turn, turn.
It's too easy. It's too accurate. It's too acute a pang
in the tooth when biting into the ice cream that melts
beside the apple pie—milk returning to its milkiness,
the land of milk and honey. And honey, the barn

is burning. Honey, the barn has burned.
And the house went crazy. And the horse went crazy.
And yonder came a man with a pencil in his hand,
a pad of paper, making notes, making adjustments,
jotting down estimates for the hole in your heart,
the hole in your horse's heart, the price of lumber,
cement, rafters, the price of something new.
So the cold weather will bring in the new. Not the new now,
the new to come, the new of one bright morning, we all look
toward something. In the high school the choir students
stand on risers—soprano, alto, tenor, bass—
O, hard times, come again no more.
It is bad music. Or good music sung badly.
But people are singing. At the October wedding
people sing along with the band, dance with the band,
they have come for the cake and the booze and to let loose,
to let loose for free, to be free to let loose, and more booze,
and a fat harvest moon rising over the backs
of their heads. Another Monday morning—the day
of the moon. The maples begin to do something amazing.
It is slow coming this year, the turning. It may come little,
it may come in late bloom, the dying is like the growing
in that we cannot project how it will turn out, we can not
call on nature to sit under our spell, to listen,
to obey. I am drinking too much coffee these days.
It is cold in the nights now, I have not yet lit
the pilot light. An old gas furnace, pretty soon I'll let it roar.
Eight hours in the car with a hangover. Four of those hours
listening to another Sunday Blues Hour. 'Twas the hour
of blues then. 'Tis the hour of silence now.
Quiet as three small doe make their way
across the field out back, and look up from the grass
and listen. So listen to the wind as it begins and ends.
Listen to the whistle at the football field.
Listen to the football coach, another bad season,
another excuse, the excuse this time being
that there is no excuse—just that none of them
care enough right now to win. From the ground up,
he says. We have to change the mentality. Change
the atmosphere. Change something. Homecoming
without much of a game to come home to.
A Hail Mary in the fourth quarter, and we all
close our eyes. And the late flowers close up
for the season. They shut down, put the plywood
over their windows. They wither and shake and moan

for a long sleep. It is easy to sleep now. It is easy not to
                get out of bed. The cold floors, the cold shower,
                        the cold breath of the cold itself on the windows.
                One more minute where it's warm. One more
        minute before I rise. But rise we must, and up
into the chill, the noise of the fall falling as a footstep falls,
        heel to toe, heel to toe, moving toward a new day.
                A small wren peeking out of a small water pail.
                        It is all precious in its smallness. It is worth more
                than its weight in gold. And the leaves go gold,
        they go for the gold, and the weight of that gold
grows heavy on their pointed shoulders, and down
            to the ground they come. Fool's gold. King's gold.
                Nature's first green as gold. This is the song of the wren
                        now. The song of two wrens, many wrens
                that sing in unison, sing in rounds, sing
        so that the song will never end. When one stops
another keeps going. When another stops the previous
        returns to take it's place. They light a fire at the everlasting altar.
                They light a fire on the porch to keep warm.
                        And in an arena somewhere in Oklahoma
                I rode an old horse named Wren. A horse so broke
        you could look in one direction, and by that small shift of looking
in your body the horse could sense where you were going
        even before you knew. A Cadillac of horses. Like driving a boat
                on open water. And with the fall wind the waves
                        on the water pick up. Choppy some days.
                Calm some days. Some days the water seems
        like a reflection. I am all for pathetic fallacies.
I am pathetic. I can take the seasons as omens, I can take
        a breeze as some voice coming over the water,
                some voice saying Yes, some voice saying No,
                        some voice saying I am the voice that speaks
                of neither yes nor no. In the backyard I smoke
        another cigarette, knowing I should not but I do
anyway, and out of the tree line a small doe comes,
        and eyes me, ears up, wanting as much as I want, it seems,
                to know the other thing. Then the mother doe comes,
                        out front of the younger, and we are all wanting
                at this point to know what to call the space between,
        the gap, the tall grass, that now grows brittle and brown.
You are safe with me, I say. Or mostly safe. I am not hungry
        today. I am not in the mood for the bitter gamey taste
                of something wild in my mouth. Domestication.
                        These deer exist between two worlds, as we all do.

Life and death. The beginning and the end.
How have we come to define these things, how can we begin
to define them, why must we, how can we not? Who, what, when,
where, why, and how, how. Howl at the harvest moon waning.
Howl at the harvest moon waxing. Hoot of the big owl
in the trees in the distance in the darkness.
The fall is a first request for forgiveness.
It is the last attempt to be stubborn.
It is something that at once hangs on
and is also resigned to let go, and in letting go
becomes something beautiful, something to break
your heart, a long drive down a gravel road
lined with trees, leaves turned and blowing
all around the motion you make, the footprint
you make, the you you make out of a moment in time and place.
Dimensions and the dementia of the dimensions.
In the nursing homes they are blessed and cursed sometimes
to forget. Forget me not. I linger in the aftertaste.
I sit on the top of the fence with my feet swinging
and wave. Wave goodbye, wave hello. Waves as they pulse
and pulse against the shoreline. Close your eyes now and you might
sleep a minute. Close them and look up to the sun, and behind
that shade make out the sun, as a bright red and blurry vision
that comes to you from the inside as it is affected
by the outside. Open those windows and look at me.
In the darkness the moon made a pattern out of the eyes
of animals dotting the field. Bright, glowing, green as they turn to me,
disappearing as they turn away. Today is Halloween. Halloween at last,
and Happy Halloween to you, my reader. I will go out into the world
soon to buy candy, something sweet just in case a child
might wander forth. Plastic pumpkins filled with bad taffy
and candy corn and quarters. Sweet, tart, salty, and savory—a sensory
overload swinging on the arm of a young girl dressed as a fairy godmother.
I could use one of those right now. I could use three wishes. I could use
the whole madness of a Halloween night—I am ready
for the whoops and hollers. In the neighbor's yard
a skeleton rising out of the ground, just in front
of a plastic gravestone. We mock what we fear. We define
what we hope for—life after death, in some way or another, even
if that life is a deathly life itself. It is the season of the zombie.
It is the season of biting necks. It is the season of brooms,
and on the stereo the blues keep playing, and they dust
that broom, for the witches to fly. Watch the moon tonight.
Watch the roads. Watch how you react to a world that for one
small moment loses its consciousness of being a world, and sets

itself free to be wild, to be fantastical, to be black and sharp and bawling
like an alley cat. In the morning, rotten teeth. In the morning
a bellyache. But tonight it is tricks and treats, tonight
they will knock on your door. History and comedy
and terror and empathy—all lined up with their hands out,
all lined up asking Please. So it pleases me. The children please me,
and the costume contest at the local bar pleases me.
They come for a free drink and to be ridiculous for one night.
They come because they've had nothing better to do,
and have worked on this costume for the past two months.
Then they leave the web, they leave the loom,
and into the tenderness of an open room, scary music
on the jukebox. Be afraid. Be very afraid. Boooooooo,
and the ghosts take flight. And again, tonight, the blood drips
from the fang. Again, tonight, the sword enters
the breast. Again, tonight, the werewolves shriek and howl,
Frankenstein walks the city streets, everything returns for the show,
the Monster Mash, as they all dance together. And what more to say
about witches blood, boiled frogs, toil and trouble. Double, double,
and Macbeth cries out: Fair is foul, and foul is fair.
I am moved tonight to let it go, to send this message
out into the darkness. The darkness tonight
becomes less, becomes lit, becomes warmed by the movement
of small feet and large feet, and giant plastic feet thumping
down the street. Welcome to your worst nightmare. Welcome
inside for something hot to drink. Welcome fall, welcome all,
you are welcome to whatever you please. So scream,
and let the scream out. And then a scream, and a wrap
on the door. Into the day of the dead we move on.
Shake the bones today, sing for the gone.
In the backyard we make a bonfire and burn
the branches that the fall has knocked back, burn
the boxes from another move, from the produce
store, burn even an old tree fallen from a September
storm, a tree too big to burn. So it chars and chars and chars.
I take the black from the bark and paint lines on my face.
In the darkness now I am cut up, camouflaged, hidden
behind a small wall of soot. And people walk by in high-top
shoes. People walk by looking for work, one more
job while the season still offers jobs—pick up sticks,
rake leaves, just sit and be there for a while.
I am here for a while. I am not going anywhere.
Hot cider and a little whisky and the sun goes down, down, down.
So the fire rises up, out of the ashes and into its own light,
crackling and popping while the sparks dance above.

It is good to be here tonight. It is good to be warm,
to be burning, to be roasting marshmallows close enough
that the hairs on my fingers singe. Smell the burning flesh.
Smell the pine wood burning. Smell the juniper in the distance—
it is the season of bathtub gin.
We sit and tell stories of ghosts and hooks
on window panes. We sit and talk and fill up
the darkness. We sit and stare as the movement of the fire
shushes us. Be quiet, he says. Hush now. So we hush
and soon it is another day. It is the same day. I am missing someone
in the ground, and I carry him with me through the weathered
grass, and up into a tree, high so that we look out across
the water. In the water the loons play hide and seek.
The mallards make a pass and then decide to move on.
In a duck blind once it was the come-back call—loud
and obnoxious with a little too much please, a little too much
don't go. Usually, they would go. Too much desperation.
Despair, ye mighty. Look down upon us now.
The big birch tree goes red now and it must
be baring its heart. How else to explain this.
The red inside as it comes to the surface now.
Another red tree in the middle of the water in the distance.
Distance as it comes, distance as it goes. I'll pull you in
close and we'll stay warm. Cold nights coming now.
Daylight savings and we all fall down.
Or fall back, one more hour, an hour earned,
a penny saved. I teach twenty young people in the mornings
about composition and on my lectern each day there are two pennies
heads up. All day long. And on and on and on.
A slow drive outside of town, where the houses
start coming less, the people start coming less, and the cattle
and horses and donkeys multiply. Go forth, you animals of the fields.
A dark man arrives to steal a mule. The mule as that sturdy ground
between smart and stubborn, solid and stout, one of the best
American traditions now traditional no longer.
Christmas decorations at the local Wal-Mart and Dollar General
and Halloween hasn't even had time to undress,
to take off its wings, and settle down with a book
next to the window as the heat kicks on. The Holidays are upon us now
and there is nothing we can do to stop it. But we can resist.
Resist the pull to put one day in front of another, resist
the pull to give-up and do it like everyone else
seems to. And they seem to know what they're doing.
They seem to have a plan. But the only plan I understand
these days is the plan to mow the yard once the leaves

have done their thing—one last pass with the mower in mulch mode,
taking them up and giving them back to the ground
in pieces. We are all in pieces. We are the fragmented
codes of a postmodern universe. But the universe
has no conception of being so. Or I say it has none,
I, who know little of the universe. On *Wheel of Fortune* the other day:
"No Man is an Island." But it is that time of year when people
set sail to exotic Caribbean locales. A little more hot sun, a beach,
cold rum. One more toast for a perpetual summer,
one more day to take the shirt off and lay down.
Here, the wind picks up, and my skin dries out.
I write messages there in white—
S.O.S's for the person that finds me here and cares
enough to read. If you have read this far than you
have read farther than most. I thank you for listening
to the strange ramblings of a man approaching
the middle of one year out of twenty-eight.
Soon to be twenty-nine, and with each year comes
a new perspective. At twenty-eight my life was easily divisible
into seven-year categories, the seven-year itch, itching
all along the sock-line again. But I am not divisible.
Or I am divided. I am a character in a word problem
somewhere, getting on a train leaving at 3:30 traveling west,
while somewhere else another character is heading my way
to meet me. The geese come now to meet me. Their migration
begins, and the ducks, too, traveling south,
popping in and out of small water holes, the banks
of large rivers. Every year they make this journey
through the perils of Mississippi and Arkansas,
a shotgun supernova in which all they remember is the pull.
So leave, return. As the leaves leave and return. The limbs
get brittle and fall and I take up the larger ones and break them
across my knee. I would build a fire
if it were legal to do so inside city limits.
I may just build a fire, anyway. Legalities.
We'll break them as well and stack them up
on the small flame as it grow larger. Burn the old chair
I hate, the bad writing of students collected in a drawer,
burn the dead tree in the yard, burn the local paper,
burn the paperboy just for delivering that paper.
I am getting out of hand. I give you the paperboy back,
I was not serious. But the red trees go up in flames themselves,
they concentrate on an image of heat or passion,
and from somewhere inside they ignite. They are the few
that take on the red this season. They are not

the green nor the brown nor the orange or yellow.
Yello?, as my dad used to answer the phone.
The yellow leaves are those that have some part
of the summer in them they still just cannot let go.
I assign meaning to the leaves. I assign specific meaning
and tomorrow I will take it all back,
or I will revise it, but today they mean these things
to me, they mean a promise, they mean good,
they mean a subtle symphony in the breeze that fills
the air with the sweet smell of the wet ground.
The last of the monarchs make their way through.
And these monarchs, I have read, are the great-
great-grandchildren of the butterflies
that left in the spring. They're going to Mexico.
It's an easy place to want to go, I've thought about going
myself many times. In the kitchen now I keep a wooden
bread bowl passed down to me from my great-great-grandmother.
A bowl that made its way once into Oklahoma
on a wagon, that returned to Missouri, and has now
traveled back to Oklahoma again. I don't know
what that means necessarily, but it's a good story,
and a good bowl. It is nice to have something
to fill up. So I fill the glass up with bourbon now.
The ice cracks as the liquor melts it down.
I rub the back of the dog who moans
a little at being rubbed—a puppy moan
and squeal because he wants to say something, but doesn't
know exactly what to say. I just say Good dog, over and over,
a refrain I repeat when he sits, stays, comes,
something I sometimes call out just when looking
at him—because he is to me, and we are
to each other, and so on. I saw on the news
the other day that a few extra pounds might
be healthy. In its abdomen the monarch stores,
relatively, a suitcase-full of fat for the trip.
I have been eating stews and root vegetables
lately. It is the time of the year for very simple foods.
This may begin to sound like a journal
of one man's seasonal eating habits. So be it.
In the backyard we dig up the carrots that didn't quite
make it. We dig them up, we unscrew the hose,
because the first frost is coming, and it comes.
Overnight the basil wilts into a sad, dark, dead version
of its former self. The mint bristles up as if all the cold did
was wake it up. I am talking about my plants like people,

58

an old, old lesson in personification. Out at the lake
　　I watch a woman edge into the freezing water,
　　　　and simply watching her makes my chest
　　collapse like a car jack quickly letting
its burden down. And Moses asks to lay his burden down.
And a man with a feed sack on his shoulder makes his way
　　to his truck to lay his burden down. The trees lay their burden
　　　　down. Down, and all around, letting it go
　　　　　with a certain joy, a certain sadness,
　　　　a certain beauty in their certainty that it is time.
　　So the time has changed. The darkness comes
an hour earlier, it has made a leap forward, a step backward,
　　it is darkness acting as the shifty thing that it is.
　　　　Before the sun comes down I stand
　　　　　and make a shadow across your face.
　　　　I am a wall between you and blindness.
　　I am the bush, burning, sent out to speak.
And in the bushes the small wrens flitter
　　and flutter. The thrushes run wild. They are quick there,
　　　　hidden there from the larger birds, the bluejays
　　　　　bullying the bird kingdom.
　　　　Kingdom come and kingdom
　　done gone. The dog sits and wags his tail.
And now you are the wag. You mean that to me.
　　In the sun and the shadow and the space between,
　　　　the darkness and the sidewalk and the way home
　　　　　past the pumpkins, an old man on a ladder
　　　　already beginning to put lights out. It is too soon,
　　I say, but I am glad he doesn't care what I say.
He is too old to care, anyway, one way or the other,
　　he is stapling long strands to the roof and wobbling,
　　　　mumbling some curse under his breath.
　　　　　Curses for the day, curses for the night.
　　　　Accursed, and I sit outside as the leaves fall
　　and smoke. A little ember and the dry remains
of one season of one tree and with the right wind
　　we could burn the world down together. Outside
　　　　town five men take sledge-hammers to the foundation
　　　　　of an old barn. I hear the bang from here.
　　　　I hear from here the pang of the bang,
　　the heart as it leaps up, lows down, lets go
of a structure soon to be no more.
　　The cattle are indifferent. They raise their heads
　　　　in unison and let the world go. They let it all go,
　　　　　and go back into the grass, growing thin now,

brown now, and how now you feel brown cow.
At the liquor store it's bourbon and chardonnay
and things to warm me up, things woody, smoky,
        things to put the fall into my mouth. I put a leaf
                into my mouth and it tastes like some sort of sweet tea,
                        something worth tasting, something strange,
                on some days I walk around the world
        like a garbage disposal. Good garbage and bad garbage.
Garbage is neither good nor bad, but only thinking makes it so.
        I have a certain aesthetic stance on junkyards.
                Outside town the old cars line up in rows, we call this
                        sometimes a graveyard but they are not dead,
                only sleeping. Waiting for something else,
        or the end, or they have no end but are only taken back,
slowly, into the ground, down, and down, and down.
        For twenty dollars you can buy a window there.
                For five they'll give you a rearview mirror.
                        But there is nothing to look back to in this place,
                the back is the story itself, you are witnessing
        the back as it has come to the present tense,
to lie and wait with the others. Then they all roll over
        and bare their beautiful backs. In the cool of the morning
                this is something to hold on to. So hold on,
                        and listen up while in the other room
                the weatherman continues to be a permanent fixture
        of households across America. Households across America,
unite. We will hold hands and rake leaves together, burn
        leaves together, despise each other together, love each other
                together, we will forever together be in flux with each other,
                        learning together, losing together, watching together
                as the wind takes the leaves down and it rains brown
        and red and yellow. The rain will come soon but today
it is the dry rain, the sweet smell of the fall's reign,
        king for one last warm day. There is something in the breeze
                now, something to feel, something that makes the horses
                        a little frisky, that gets the dog to run in circles
                around the tree, it is nothing that can be explained
        but it is witnessed everywhere, felt everywhere, found
everywhere in small examples of people shivering,
        people skipping, people shaking hands and saying hello
                like they mean it this time, and they do mean it today,
                        today is a day for meaning.
                So what have I come to mean to you? You me,
        he she, vice versa and what do we mean together?
The sun cuts through the tree first,

and then the window, and across the floor
		it paints a shadow of leaves shaking, leaves falling,
				leaves dancing behind the screen for a little exhibition
		showing one night only. And one night is what we have
	tonight, so we will make it last. We will
take the night and hold it against each other,
	we will breathe there, hard there, under stars
		as the weather shakes out the background.
				And in the distance I hear the football game,
		the crowd cheering, the crowd weeping,
	the band recording that emotion in percussion
and brass. The season is wearing on the bodies now,
	it is coming to a head. The players sit after practice
		in the locker rooms, icing a shoulder, dipping their bodies
			back and forth into the cold whirlpool
		and the hot whirlpool—it is the time now
	again for healing. The pads have taken on
the sour smell of a season, war wounds, the helmets
	marked with the paint of seven other teams.
		A history of violence, a history of good sportsmanship,
			a history of hard work, lessons learned, lesson unlearned,
		long days and long nights after the games
	spent drinking cold beer in the cold night
with cold hands holding the waist of somebody warm.
	The cold hands of death upon you. A startle, a shake, a shiver
		and then the cold melts into the warmth, they melt
				into each other, they become one another
		for a moment under the new moon,
	bodies and truck beds and curfews looming.
They look up, and see a falling star. It has fallen
	for them. It has fallen for the fall. It has fallen
		as evidence that this moment is marked, it has been
				noted, documented, recorded in the cosmic
		cabinet of all such events. We supply the destiny to destiny.
	Or else it just waits for us to see. We are not to know,
and I am not for the knowing. I am for the mystery.
	The gray owl swooping across the field, and back
		into the shadows of the trees at the edge.
				The abrupt edge, the home today of a thousand birds.
		The birds sense the cold, they sense, too,
	in the warmth the horse's whinny, the dog's bark,
the little buck of a donkey feeling alright, feeling fine,
	feeling good enough today to break her back.
		Another Sunday at the horse tracks and people
				come out today because the season will soon

be over, and the thoroughbreds will return to their homes
in Oklahoma and Texas and Kentucky, they will shake off
the season and put on a little weight. It is a good time to gamble,
while there is still gambling to be done, before
the money saved will go to buy Christmas presents,
tickets home for the holidays, stuffed animals
that sing carols over and over at the local pharmacy.
Dear Pharmacist, fill this please. A drug
for the good days, a drug for the bad days.
A drug for old age, older age, aging, dying,
a drug, a drug, a drug. The fall afternoon
is its own drug. Soon the turkey drug,
and in the living room bodies downed
as if some sleeping gas had been let loose
in the house, grown men in socks, grown women
drooling, all the grown-ups already thinking of eating
too much, of one thing out of many
for which they give thanks.
And today we give thanks for the wind.
Forty miles per hour, fifty, a strong push
to bring the leaves down, bring the house down,
raise the roof and we are humming and electric.
The fan on the floor pushes the back of the shirt
off the hanger. At the local airport
a group of flight students sit around
an old propeller, smoking, telling stories,
each with a tale of the time they almost died:
I looked Death in the face, I stared him down as he lifted
off the runway and up to me like a body coming
out of the water, risen from the grave,
it was Death and me and a little Cessna,
I hollered out for my mother in the cab
but no one was there to hear. But they all hear it now,
they hear it as they each have heard it before, as they hear it
in their own versions, their own fears, their own
push forward, the wind that pushes, that takes the plane
as it wants to, when it wants to, the wind that the white hands
pull against. Today's calendar saying: You can never go back.
There is no back there. No there there. There-there, now,
lay your head down and purr. There are versions, there is just
the one version, the one you are living, but also the versions
you live in your head, sometimes these become the same
versions, you become the one person, the version
of the one person you had held somewhere
for a long, long time. Cushing, Oklahoma and I stop in

to the Steak Inn. A place where the steaks come to hang
their hats, escape the reality of being a steak, being real,
being cooped up so long in the house of a big black cow.
And on I-35 people are on the road. Every day
people are on the road. If there were no people
the road would cease to exist, but it exists, and it exists here
where it cuts across I-44 north of Oklahoma City, as I-44
cuts across and around and becomes Rt. 66, the mother road,
the road that holds us and feeds us and slows us down,
as we look and see our faces in the reflection
of a silver diner, a deal on hot dogs, fried-onion burgers,
sweet potato and pumpkin pie for the hungry,
and today they have made real whipped cream.
So the heavy cream gets heavier in the mixer.
A wire whisk and sugar and you have yourself
a magic trick. The leaves do their magic,
they disappear. They shimmy and shake behind the sheet,
and then Poof!, abracadabra, they're gone.
And as the leaves shed themselves the birds
feel their nakedness, and for a short time bask
in that nakedness—to be so open and bare
and in the treetop, sing. Sing-whistle, diddle-diddle,
soon the wind will turn. It is turning today. It is turning
on us all. It comes around from the south, then west, then north
of northwest—cold and clinging to my face with a slight mist.
Come the sunshine again, come the rain again.
Two promises I can make to you.
Across from the mall I sit in an old diner
and eat fried chicken and biscuits and fries
out of a red basket. Beverly's Pancake Corner, the last
holdout of Chicken-in-the-Rough. This is a landmark,
but not marked, nor even known by most that pass
around it. The first fast food, when fast food still meant
good food, and it is good today and hot
on the roof of my mouth—four o'clock closing time as the sun
comes through the metal blinds. And I am blinded
by the light. I am Manfred Mann on the radio station,
the DJ's knowledge of history and trivia and tried and true
ways of dealing with the workday. Five o'clock comes
and we all fall down. Down and out, and into the arms
of a happy hour, a big, soft chair, a television show
and then sleep and dreams and tomorrow and again
and again. Again and again and again. A slight gain
on death, a slight gain on life, a slight gain on the mortgage,
the car payment, the degree, the trip to the West Indies.

Sugar and spice and everything nice. It is the season now
of Cinnamon. A stick ground to a powder, a powder
placed in a pie, a palette for the food and the fed, and the need
and want for the finality of that last bite.
We are training now. We are stretching our stomachs
for the holiday season. Binge-calisthenics,
I can't stop thinking about heart attacks.
In a house down the road from the house
I grew up in, a man hung himself in a tree
on Halloween day. This is me looking back.
All day long he hung and people walked by
and children walked by, perhaps each thinking
What a strange but real decoration.
So we decorate. We deck the halls. We parody
the parody of life as a man hung in a tree on the holiday
when so many things hang from trees on holidays. And the leaves still hang
from the trees, but today the wind blows them down,
it blows it all down, and him down, as he stretches
the rope and gets loose to be gone, So long
and long gone, he floats into memory in a dark
flannel shirt. It is the season of furry sheets. The season
of down comforters. The season of comfort if comfort
can be said to be a thing one can offer, it is offered,
it is held out on a paper plate heavy and burdened
by eyes bigger than appetites, appetites bigger
than themselves, it is held out to the homeless and hungry
and full and full-of-themselves, it is offered, it is taken,
took down as a sacrifice—a fire to the wind, a man to the wind,
a child to the wind like a leaf let go, blown on through
a tan pasture, over a tanned cattle hide, on and on
into another story of another time, until it is time
to go to work again, as the alarm goes off
in your head before you hear it going off
in reality—you have come now to see the future.
And the future is a thing that can be seen. On television
the football commentators look forward
to the Super Bowl, bowl games, they make predictions
and stake their lives on their claims, they realize
the absurdity of their claims, they speak
with broad shoulders and moustaches in coats and ties
and say profound things: The past is history,
the future is a mystery, today is a gift
and that is why it's called the present.
And on commercial breaks Christmas is in blossom,
garlands and green and red and white covering

every inch of every image of the screen. But now
is the time to give thanks. So give thanks
for the early-bird specials, a hot plate
and a good salad bar, soup to warm your soul.
Give thanks for the pumpkin pie brought you,
the right thing at the right time, and all the rightness
of the world still struggling to right itself. Give thanks
for the mule deer, the buck, give thanks.
Give thanks for the brandy and bourbon
and wine held in hands before the dinner,
after the dinner, give thanks for the warmth, the mirth,
the cold spell between one human and another, the liquor
that heats them up. Give thanks for the candlelight,
the fire on the porch, the fire burning down
an old hotel in Tulsa tonight, give thanks
for all the memories that burn
and the memories that do not burn, burn
and burn for the memory in which you currently reside.
Give thanks for the man, the woman, the dog, the horse.
You have been brought here to be thankful,
we are gathered today to reflect,
as the turkey reflects on a life well-lived,
a life poorly lived, a life not lived at all but give thanks
for the turkey that has given its life. Give thanks and sacrifice.
Give thanks and pray. Give thanks and eat, dig in, devour.
The world on a platter, it's never that easy, it's not going
to ever be that easy, but give thanks
that on some days it is precisely that easy,
even easier, give thanks, give thanks for the morning fog.
And on the ground the bluejays and squirrels quarrel
over the pecans, thankful for the pecans today,
we are all so thankful, all supposed to be so thankful,
so take a moment to get away from the Christmas
to come—it will come, it will come, give thanks
for the thanking holiday of the in-between.
Neither here nor there, not quite, almost,
the Pilgrims and the Indians pose for a black and white photo.
This is old-fashioned anymore. Just dinner and a table.
Give thanks for the table, the eaves of the table,
the extra chair, the extra plate, the extra time
of a Thursday and Friday to eat a little extra, mope
a little extra, as the extra-terrestrials fly through the night,
staring at the celestial light of the moon and giving thanks
for one moon among many moons, our moon, just mine
and yours, we will look on it tonight and be near

each other, a long rope swung over the top
and tugging a little on us throughout the day, feeling
the other, and the weight of the moon, and the gravity
as it keeps the table-settings in places.
A family gathered in Mississippi, and the little ones
spell out the name, crooked letter, crooked letter.
I take a drive with my brother-in-law, past the cotton
gins, the mounds of hulls, past the grave of Fanny Lou Hamer,
past an enormous hunting lodge, and on to a small farm
where we check the water level, the rain that has come
but not come enough. And the rain, the rain, the rain.
A delay in the Atlanta airport. Thousands of people
just wanting to get back home, and some
from Akron, Ohio, wanting to get back home
bad enough they will lose their manners for one quick moment
and levitate as small bodies of heat in front of the airline help desk.
I come to the help desk for help. Help!
All Elvis wants to do is shake. All John Lee
wants to do is boogie. All I want to do is get out
of this airport, home to another airport, the first snow
coming down in Oklahoma City. A few days ago,
Black Friday signaled the beginning of Christmas,
men and women and children lined outside the doors
of Wal-Mart, four in the morning, waiting
for the deals of the year, waiting to go crazy.
And Oklahoma is one-hundred years old this November,
one-hundred years since early settlers lined up with their horses
and wagons, hitched to a dream of free land, a better tomorrow,
the ease of some politician's thumbs running inside
his suspenders. In time, we suspend. Our pants,
we suspend. The rebellious teens at the high school,
they suspend. And the earth is suspended by a poor theory
of physics. On Friday the fall ends. Even though the leaves
are just turning in Atlanta, the people have turned. Even though
winter will not officially begin until December 23rd, it has
officially begun in the hearts of thousands of Americans,
putting out their stockings, their Christmas decorations,
even as the turkey stays good in the refrigerator.
It's cooling off now. Lordy, it's cold. The wind turns
from the south and comes out of the north, it comes hard,
pulsating, shaking the last of the brittle brown
from the trees. And we be the trees. We be shook.
We be ready for something else, not ready to leave
something else, we be the in-between, the betwixt,
twitching on a branch as it moves. Let go, and move on.

Y'all come see us again. In the background of this narrative
a football game is on. And they are playing for much more now.
They are playing their last game, the game to propel them
to a better game, a pointless game, a championship game,
they are laying everything on the line because when the season is over
it is over, and there is no returning. The fall will come back
but you cannot, yourself, return to the fall. So we wait
for what's to come. We hope we will see it all come again.
It has been lovely and singular. It has been
a season of record. When the cleats leave the edge
of the field they may or may not ever touch that ground again.
The leaves grow brown and down into the ground.
On some days, wet. On other days, they crumble.
And it is from that dust they rise. And to dust they now return.

III. THE ICEHOUSE

Thirty degrees and the power goes out.
                    Ice on the lines.   Ice covering the roads.
          The great ice storm of ought seven
and the world   today   is frozen   stiff. A quarter inch
          blanketing the tree limbs like some translucent gauze
a stiff cast   gone wet   then solid   then brittle
                    and then broken.   A giant limb comes tumbling
from the top   and on   and down   to the ground.
          Even the barbed wire is covered, so that there are no barbs today
only the cold sting   of dry skin   touching water in its solid state,
          water stood upright in the image of man, carved out into an angel
for a wedding reception   in some cold Elk's lodge of northern Illinois.
There is no noise in Illinois   only silence
          and silence   distracted, as another something   breaks its frozen heart
and covers that heart again   or else, just begins to melt.
There are fourteen solid phases of water.
          And in each crystal there is a narrative of beauty   of death
of the history of water as it sprung once   from the eternal well
          leapt up to behold   and then a world gone cold   and then the people
all got thirsty.   A big block of ice coming in on the ice wagon.
          A body laid out and kept   until the ground thaws
enough to dig.   So dig deeper, and watch your step.   It is the season
of broken hips, broken limbs, broken interpretations of the summer.
          Winter, and your lips are dry.   Winter, no longer the striptease
of fall   but the woman   the man left naked and revealed.
          But today the ice conceals. Or does not conceal
it puts on display, it is a window through which we look, and downtown
tonight   fifteen children sit inside a corner store with banjos
          wearing Santa Claus hats, and playing a winter jig. And because they all miss
the note they come to represent the note   they play a new note
a strange and eerie note   blared outside on speakers as we look in
                    and on   and they out   to such a long line of lookers.
          This morning the trees feel the same. Because there is something
between our looking they are made aware of the looking, of the look
          they grow away and droop the weight of so much water
on their shoulders   so much precipitation   so much of a season
                    so being in winter   they are wintered to the root   cold to the bone
          until it too rings out some odd and longing pang of song.
A quarter-cord of wood frozen stiff   but inside   the fire burns.
In the next episode   the world melts. But from where that melting springs
          I cannot safely say.   Does the tree will it so from within?

Does the water re-write its story once again?   Tune-in next week
          and I'll offer you my hand.   So we sit around the radio and watch
as the logs flicker and spit their ash to the sky.   They spit their ash
          out and onto the carpet   they spit their ash so that they might burn.
I drink hot tea   hot chocolate with schnapps   bourbon cider
anything to try and keep warm   or away—something to keep my own water
          moving. Outside the birdbath is frozen, and on the rim
a chickadee begging for a drink.   Or else it is the mockingbird
          come back to mock all the other birds   and guard its sacred ground.
It is black on white on gray on ice. It is a cold, wet color scale.
On Main Street a Christmas parade   full of all the hope and sadness
     of Christmas.   We are all within Christmas now, the holiday season
there is no outside of it   there is no escape. So give into it
          or hole-up and scrooge yourself past and on and into a new year.
The new year is coming. A new day is dawning. But today the dawn is covered
          in gray   and ice   and garland   and colored lights.
A parade for every season, and the seasons together as their own parade.
          So sit tight. Bundle up. Crawl deep into the folds of your scarf,
your down comforter, your fire, your cider, your version of keeping warm
in a cold time.   Let the festivities begin.   And they will begin
whether you want them to or not.   Guthrie, OK
          and they are dressing up in Victorian garb for the season.
Women in windows making quilts and baking apple pies.
          Men in windows dressed as cowboys long at work on a poker game.
This is the simulation   and the space between   the simulation
and reality.   We are almost real tonight.   We are too real.
          We are some fantasy come to life, sitting in the Blue Bell Saloon
having drinks where the old silent-film star Tom Mix once served cocktails.
This is not supposed to make any sense   necessarily.
          We are only as necessary tonight   as the bourbon is necessary
the ice in the bourbon necessary   the wind outside bringing more ice
for everyone   bad roads for everyone   and then I hold my hands
          to my mouth and blow   and blow out some version
of a much warmer story   the heat as it hits my face just coming in
          through the doorway.   So if Ifs and Buts were candy and nuts
then we'd all have a Merry Christmas.   Merry Christmas, baby.
          They're wishing it well at the grocery store. They're wishing it well
at the coffee shop. Happy Holidays, all you people, they're wishing it well.
          Even as the wishing well freezes over.   And in the wishing well
the coins put to their best use.   They are the arbitrary tokens
          of much more than a monetary system.   They are the faces
of presidents laden with the hope of one human   closing their eyes
          and letting their dreams out into wherever dreams come from
wherever they go, however they be, what they do, when they do, what they do.
A desk and a pencil and a Christmas list begins.   You've been naughty

you've been nice. You've been considering
the meaning of both.   The rain drizzles. It has come
      to melt the ice.   To melt the ice   and become the ice.
At this moment the water outside is having a long conversation
         about its destiny, composition, purpose in this the coldest season.
So the season of death, supplied with so many metaphors.
         No leaves, no flowers, and we put so much pressure on the evergreens.
Put a bird on the bough. An ornament set to sing. Fill it with lights
      and the hope   of a white Christmas.   The radio
is playing the tune.   We exist somewhere in the melody.   Annoyed
at the same old songs   happy to hear the same old songs   once more,
      it is all new this year   it is all beginning again   so put your coat on
and your gloves and hat   because friends   'tis the season
      known as the season—the one that wears its heart on its frozen sleeve.
Then how you get there   thawed.   Coleslaw
      and the Christmas ham.   The winter equinox   a day
that comes without much coming. And come   they told him
      pa rum puh-pum pum.   We gather as families for the holidays.
As separate entities   conjoined   by blood, love, law, loss.
We feast on the sweet things   we trade the sweet things   we offer
      the sweet things in Christmas tins in exchange for sausage and cheese
and boiled custard.   A double boiler   a bowl of cracked eggs.
Sugar, baby, sweety, hun. Sorghum for breakfast. Maple syrup for lunch.
      This is a caloric celebration   where we put on the winter weight
and then wait   and then hibernate   until the new year comes
      and we resolve to do at least one   of several things   better.
On the mantle a teddy bear   reading some Christmas tale
for the children.   And the anticipation   of the children
      of a bearded man   a bellied man   a candyman
come down the chimney   to fulfill their dreams   to butcher their dreams
      to eat another cookie with a tall glass of milk.   The morning
comes early. The late night before, drinking homemade wine   we call brandy
      drinking bourbon while making gingerbread cookies   the spice of life
too much, a little more, why yes I'll have another glass   I'm not driving
      I'm not working tomorrow   I'm not doing anything   but waiting
      for the world to proceed before me.   And it proceeds.
         On Saturday I go to an enormous store to buy things in bulk
I sit and wait   with the others there   for free samples of food.
      I reach into a pot of chicken wings with a toothpick while some old woman
         with a shower cap on slaps my hand   and shoos me away.
Shoo now   and sweep the devil out with the new year.   At some point
      this winter they will light small candles at churches across the land
and shut down the lights   and sing.   A silent night
to proceed another eve.   The season of eves.   Of anticipations, moments before
      days before   because the days of   are always the days of

and so the night before we drink   and dance   and I sit with the dog
          and watch the ball go down on t.v.   And this a poem about years.
One year.   A long year.   A year that seemed   at times
          to fly   as the owl flies at night   swooping across my face
and filling me with fear   and wonder   and hope
          as the pores of my flesh rise   to meet that fear   to meet
another year   and more hope   more promise
          more   and more   anticipation.   A season of driving.
Going home   coming home   hauling with the heater on high
through brown fields   then fields lightly covered with snow
          then cars bringing a heavier snow   on their hoods and roofs
down from Kansas or northern Missouri.   And outside a gas station
a patch of ice   a slick spot   I maneuver around with my coffee
          a bad version of a double-cheeseburger   something big and meaty
to share with the dog who rides with me.   We are moving on.
          We are wearing our new year's hats and blowing on kazoos.
It is cold out.   Cold and so still.   The electric heater
          goes on and then throws a breaker and in the cold
and in the stillness   with a flashlight he comes   to save us all.
          Across Oklahoma the power stays out   in places
from the ice.   It is ice no more   it is almost seventy degrees
          but in the history of this ice   in its narrative   are long
repercussions   lasting effects   changes and changes
          changing changes   forever. So the people go to the local bars
          and drown whatever they must drown   together.
          They take a strong hand   and take it down under the liquid
and squeeze the life   out of some dream   or hope or the antithesis
          until it stops shaking   and is still.   And when it is still
          a dollar in the jukebox   a long look at the karaoke catalogue
searching for the right song   for the right moment   which is now
          and always now   and never anything else.
The downtown puts its Christmas decorations out   and the downtown
          takes its Christmas decorations down.   And the downtown plays
holiday music   and then no music at all.   Or perhaps
some local station   playing the sort of music that is   itself
          about downtowns   and downtown people   and the misery
                    and joy   and wonderment of a night spent downtown
          at a downtown station   too drunk and playing cards   in a holding cell
with some fellow from Iowa   who only came here   to see
          a woman   but in seeing her has been witness to much more.
And so they come   and go   the ghosts
          of Christmas past   present   future
          and the scythe of time comes down upon us all   the harvest
a bygone thing   the crop a bygone thing   the winter wheat
          coming up green today   on a green day   an early warm day

promising spring but promising it   with a seasonal handicap
as the wasps and bees and frogs shake themselves out of a deep sleep for one moment
        by all indications it is a time to be alive.   So live   and live knowing
that it will grow cold again   but that today it is not   today is a gift
            this has been said by the masses   held tight by the millions
when the gifts are gone we grow aware now of the gift of life   such a cliché
such an easy explanation   for a world in which easy explanations   fail
        in which language   often fails   and people fail   and fall
but it is a day to stand up and try once more.   So a foot in the stirrup
        and the cowboy rides again.   Give us more buck, more madness
more of the horse that refuses to take to the bit   and a bit more of that
        give us the struggle of a cold winter chancing to be kind   today
springing to life again for a moment   being too much
        in that moment   as the roots take hold and shoot upward
        as the weather gives them reason enough today to press on.
And the Epiphany   and the end to lights   across town
the white Victorian house   with lights from head to toe playing along
        with a Christmas instrumental   like some giant, organic equalizer
set to map out the movement of song.   And then a small, dirty
one-bedroom with a manger scene in the front window   and Mary and Joseph
        the baby Jesus lit in plastic   a simple sort of beauty
warmth   the curtains pulled back   and the story coming down.
Into the boxes   into the shed.   Return and wait for the return again.
        I take a long ride in a pick-up with my friend   out to his farm
where a battery charger continually hums, warming up a new sprayer
and a small cat with a bobbed tail curls up in a busted chair
                beside a wood heater   and purrs.   Outside
the smoke rises to the sky   and the clouds do something   magnificent
they are mountains today   rolling across this the Mississippi Delta horizon
        a faint rainbow   shotguns in the distance   ten-thousand snow geese
upon ten-thousand snow geese   a legion of speckled white covering the sky
        up high   and down low   the red-tailed hawk   the chicken hawk
the hawk as persistent symbol   season in   and season out
        he sits on the high wire and cocks his head as we go by.
Cheeseburgers and coffee.   A talk about our lives, his new child
getting bigger   growing stronger   punching
        my divorce   his brother   our fathers   and his father's knee
surgery, where they'll saw the bone straight through on both sides   and replace
the entire thing. And so there, that day, it was cooler   not cold
        but I wondered in my head   the feel of new knee   on a cold day
and the pain of the surgery   the pain of the rehab   all that pain
        to lead to a day when that knee hurts no more   and he walks upright again
with a straight back, steady, and on into a tall row of corn.   Then back
in Oklahoma I take the dog for a long walk to witness the winter   and wonder
its nature   its season   a Sunday morning wherein some church in America

they sing "I wonder as I wander"   and I wander   and the hymn
goes through my head   my sanctuary   the woods   an armadillo
     sharing the trail   as it prays   today   for a kind soul   in return
for armor   armored against the cold.   And we take sticks and throw them
     on the ice   the frozen ponds   just to listen to the echo   of the water
underneath   the sound that wood makes   on glass   on depth
     percussion   and repercussion   an eerie sound   and comforting, too
          as the large owl hoots again somewhere in the distance.
I am human today.   How else to explain this.   It is a new year
     and I have eaten my black-eyed peas   cooked with hog jowl
this is to be an outward sign   of inward humility   an omen of good
     luck   am I lucky   am I humble   how the moon sometimes
becomes just a sliver   of itself   but beyond that sliver
     we sense   we see   the whole.   Hold on to your dreams.
I say this, I mean this, it is a simple thing to say, but hold on.   In the ice storm
     hold on. In the warmth of an early January day, a record-setting
temperature, hold on, and hold on, and hold on.   What to make of it all
the good and the bad   knowing that sometimes I can do   a terrible thing
just to know   I have done   a terrible thing.   And terror rides
     on black coattails   it rides with the cold wind   the north wind
it rides with awe and beauty and wonder and fear and death and night and day and never
     never knowing anything for sure   but knowing some things without doubt
without reservations   and letting loose into the terror and joy of living
another day.   I am nostalgic about days on this January 7, 2008   a day
     after my father had a heart-attack   as he heals even now   doing better
but the symbol has shook   as my own heart shook   and so it is a day
in which to pronounce: I am mortal.   The obvious   of course.   But it is
     the obvious as the winter makes it obvious   as the limbs
bare themselves   to the ice   the warmth   the wind   and creak
     in the distance like an old, metal gate   swung open to let the horse in
to drink   to eat   to turn its hips toward the wind   and hunker.
     In the winter   it is said   that mostly things are dead
killed by the cold   or else   mutely alive   the various forms:
     egg   seed   pupa   spore.   But nothing dies as such but rather
learns in this season   to live   a different way
to breathe   a different way   as the turtle that sucks oxygen out of the water
     and into the blood   the frogs frozen underground   that take the air in
through their skin   a butterfly   persisting   hidden in the bark of a tree.
     So we knock on the bark and say Hello.   And you bark
against the cold air   the warm air   you bark as your own means of breathing.
And a season of holidays settles into a season of not knowing where it is
     or who it is   exactly   a spot between two well-known places
to warm places   warm memories between life and death   gift and gift
     and in this gray limbo it becomes its own gift   a time given to us all
the time in which I was born   the season from which I swam   and out

and up   to breathe in the wild air of January   to take the benevolence
of a world   barren enough   that it offers itself   fragile
vulnerable   the beginnings   now   of a season of new beginnings.
And then we wade into the lake   the cold   chancing against the chance
of sickness   the pang of the iciness   chancing against reason
because that is reason enough to go in   slow   then under   and up
to where the chest closes on itself   and makes known the feeling
of a heart stopped   a heart pressing on   a heart held inside
a body   a heart holding that body up   all around it   the heart
that is the heart   the heart   the heart.   I drink too much coffee
and the chimes in the carport   map out a north-wind song.
It come down from Minnesota.   It come down from Wichita.
It come down from a place unknown   a pattern unknown   it come
from the great well of the coming.   The warm days   have gone
for now. For now the days are the in-between, fifty degrees
partly cloudy   partly windy   parting the part of a tall man
in corduroy   parting the space between and holding everything still
for a moment   moving it again   a moment later   this magic moment
so much a song about Keats   and where is Keats   in the winter
except everywhere.   To stand beside a red bucket   and ring a bell
the bell itself   begging for change.   And the Salvation Army come
to save us all.   Sometimes giving   itself   is an act of
salvation.
How to speak of salvation.   How to speak of ripeness, newness, metamorphosis
against the outward signs of stasis.   There is a constant flux
as down the road a young child learns to tie his shoes   as the mother
sits inside and for the first time   moves past the clothing catalogue   the kitchen
catalogue   and on and into some brochure   selling an escape.
The catalogue of catalogues.   The bay horse   blue heeler
pack of coyotes yipping in the distance   children yipping men hollering
hot wings and football   playoffs bowl games   championships
and champions   a bowling alley   full of men   sitting at this point
proud of their bellies   their balls   their shoes   their night out
in sweatpants   and overalls   in beer   and plastic chairs
the women at home   proud   to get rid of those men   for a night
the narrative of everything between being there   and being gone
and knowing and not knowing   the new semester the bells
marking the time again   the policeman   the squad car
the glass of bourbon sweating a ring into the coffee table   and the ring
lost   gone   the muffler   rattling   the muffler   worn
by some grandmother   before going out the lights going out   and coming
on   flickering   the itty-bitties at the bingo hall   the chance   the hope
in numbers and ink   the voice of an old fellow who once sang Sinatra
to a hundred young women and meant it   and was loved for it   that voice
still holding that passion somewhere   even as it calls out   B-12

A-7   R-13   Q-22   and Bingo   someone has it   and Bingo
we have come for it all   Bingo   your life and Bingo   your bang
    and Bingo in the trees   and beach blanket Bingo   and Bingo
for the pattern coming together   and Bingo for being here today   tonight
Bingo for a carryover jackpot   two-thousand dollars   a ham for Sunday
    pineapples and glaze   honey   honey mustard
with cherries on top.   There is the change of the season   the changes within
the seasons   there is the constancy   of the seasons   and of humans
    people   persons not to be confused with biology
or psychology   or the entire family of ologies   they are real   we are all real
and un-reducible   indescribable   often unknowable more
    than matter   matter that matters   and how comes the long tale of one single
individual   how long the fire that burns while he speaks   while she speaks
    how much wood to keep that fire   to hear that story   what tree
gives its life in essence   for a tale   a tale told   in all truth
but not all true   is any of this even worth the paper on which I write   a question
    to ask   and a question I ask myself often.   But it must be asked
because in making something   I am taking something   giving
    something   and sometimes   giving and taking so much.
And the winter gives everything   to the ground   it takes the fall in
    it takes it under   it feeds   it fuels   it falls alone in the woods
somewhere   and is harvested   and burned   and crackles
where we sit around a small circle of stones and inside the fire burns
    while someone   soon   will open up   thawed out
        and once blossomed there   where little else blossoms
begin to speak.   In New Hampshire   the politicians speak
    the primaries   a warm day there, too   warm for the handshakes
the thousands   the ten-thousands   the handshakes
offered as promise   as return   investment in human flesh   human
    ideology human hope   and I am trying today
to care.   It is often hard for me   to care about these things.
I turn the news on and it hums   in the background   I eat crackers
    and share them with the dog   and this seems more important   to me
than anything else at the time   any flat tax   Medicare   healthcare
minute change in the war   any promise   any stance on terrorism
I am trying   trying   trying   but it all seems so far away
    it is all
    far away   undecided   and not soon to be decided   the information
that drifts through the trees   with the robins   as I walk through the woods
    and with them share the blue berries   of a red cedar.   This is one way
that I get my gin fix.   Other times   I go straight for the gin.
    And the cotton gins in Mississippi grow cold these days   barren   the tin
and metal   waiting   to go to work again   and I have gone to work again
    adjusting to the pattern of another year.   And so another year begins to close
itself around me hug me   hold me   squeeze me and even

78

squeeze the life out of me and give that life back   another year
another day   another dollar   and outside   the wild squalor
of the squirrels going at it in the trees   and now the he-male cardinal
        goes red and changes his song   taking on that redness
        highlighted against the bleak foliage   he is singing sweet these days   he wants
something else these days more than food   more than territory
        more than anything he wants to be loved   however you want to define
love   in this context   this situation   perhaps it is a fallacy
to supply emotion   to the birds   but this is a fallacy   I will
fall
        right into.   And so Mr. President   Mrs. President
who will it be   what will it be   what you gonna do for me what do you
        kind sir   kind ma'am   what do you believe   and believe
way down deep there when the lights go down   what is it you cling to
        at night   through the nightmare   through the late-night telephone call
        that is not the news you wanted to hear   not the news at all
as you have seen it   over   and over   as it follows your every move
but something else   something close sad   hard   bad   my question
        for you all tonight   is how do you cope   with being alive.
The answers fail and fall into pattern   of platform   and anti-platform
and solid phrases that they believe make the American heart well.   But we are not
        welling   or I am not welling   it is important   to me
to collect the undesirable information of your soul.   But who wants to know
        these things, really.   The winter asks nothing of me
only that I hold out   for its work   only that I give it that much credit
that in its coldness it holds a plan that in its reservations   it holds a plan
        that in its shoulder turned away   its head not turning back
that even in the silhouette of its muscular back   it has not forgotten me.
And so sometimes we must embrace   the un-embraceable   and wait
        and hold   for the work held underneath   the labor   gone
unnoticed   the thousand promises   written ten-thousand times   across
one state   after another   at last unfolded   and revealed
        as on a cool sunny day   like today   the birds return
to the trees   and fill that void and bustle   and sing a song
        for one another   and sing a song   for us   and sing a song
of what is still left   what is still   and what is someday   the leaves to
come.
Two days of frost   and the temperature   rises.
        Rise from your grave, ye of the past.   Rise up into the present.
The dew point   the crystals   not a killing frost
because there is nothing much   right now   to kill.   So let it
        live   or else   think about living again   in the future
but the frost comes down   it rises up   it comes from nowhere, really
        the air already there   the substance   already there   it is water   as it is
always water   waiting for the temperature   to change   the form to change

waiting for a small structural grammatics   saying Do this
and then this   and this   follow my lead into beauty
its several manifestations.   The planes buzz overhead
          from the local airport   making passing rounds   a constancy
of my day   when there is no constancy   in the Oklahoma weather
     no constancy   in the frost   as it melts   evaporates   goes back
     to whatever that place is from which it came.   An invisibility cloak
and Poof!   I'm gone   and here   and neither here   nor gone
     but changing states   from one moment   to the next.
          On a clear day   the small jets paint their memory across the sky
white lines   demarcations   road signals   to pass
not pass   and for one brief moment   I remember being young and listening
     to Ricky Van Shelton   of all people   sing Keep it between the lines
which meant leeway   a bit   constraint   a bit   today   to tell you the truth
I'm not exactly sure   what it meant   or means   but the tune
     I remember.   It is a winter unlike itself today.   I have few winter things
     to report.   The weathermen   the weatherwomen
are happy, locally, to not report on these things   but globally   they report
     of record snows in New England   record snows also reported by Donald Hall
          record snow reported in the poems being written even now
by some New England woman   man   someone cold and gone inside
     a hot cup of tea   a blanket   an old typewriter and I look out
while still the birds sing.   It is a strange year   weatherwize
     and otherwise.   Early tornados are cutting across America   America
          southern Mississippi   where my youngest sister
     sells medical equipment   near Jackson   near Vicksburg   tornados
in Wisconsin   but not yet   touching down   in Oklahoma   with our pride
in said tornados   our pride in the wild wind that whips   and whirs
     your hair into some mad bird's nest a bird with more mad vision
than sense   a bird of the beautiful and absurd and loose things   but careful
     too   to not lose its blue eggs   careful in twos   careful
     beside a small body of water   amidst the robins   a robin itself but not
robin-ish   a small creature that sits and watches what the cattails do
     which is to signify   what else   an environment in transition
cattails   just stalks now   but still working to dry up a piece of land
as their roots   go like roots   and turn water into solid ground.
     Natural   and magnificent and wondrous   and sad, too
     to lose that water sad to lose the fish that swam through that water
the fish that breathed   the fish that flopped   the fish gone down into the mud
and into a small bone cake   an exhibit for some eighth-grade biology glass case
     witness the world   you little fools   and love it   right now
for all of its strangeness. In Tulsa we pull into the White River Fish Market
     to come   like the others   for the fish pulled out of some other place
the ocean   a trout pond   catfish farm   where the ruddy ducks
make a temporary home.   January and the beginning of the end

of duck hunts   rice fields   flooded corn stubble   dark cypress
and the end   of the shotguns   echoing across the water
        of one of the local lakes.   Hip-waders hung out to dry   patched   placed
in the tool shed for the spiders when they come again   as they will come again
as all will soon come again   in the distance   the days ahead   even
now
        as the clover makes itself brave   knowing the strength of the Bermuda
     in the heat   the wildness of the fescue in the spring   knowing now
in the time of death   is the moment to rise up   now is the time to take root
to fight   the small and cosmic fight fought every year.   In a pasture
     near my home a small cow has freed itself   not knowing how   or why
but recognizing itself as a cow on the other side   and in knowing this
allowing itself the freedom to stay   with the others   the freedom
     of a reckless eye a knowing eye   a patch of grass directly across
          from another cow   it has known well all these years   in its infancy
and now as a young adult. I speak of the cattle like children.   And the children
speak of the cattle like siblings.   And the Sibyl speaks   the unspeakable things
known through hearsay   through what has come to be   through the thousand
prophecies she has seen come true.   Perhaps in speaking these things
     she is the one who makes them so   perhaps in speaking
these things   she is more or less god   perhaps   perhaps not   perhaps
     the winter forces me into a certain type   of recollection   a certain type
          of question   perhaps the whiskey   perhaps the gin
perhaps the jukebox   playing a dirty song   for a dirty bar   as we take
     our pool sticks and knock knock   knock   the lights out.
I got some kind of faith   in some kind   of something.   In the news
I read that the plague is making a comeback   and why not.
     Today is a day unlike other days   insomuch as the narrative arc
          of its passing   the slow warming   the slow cooling
is slowly being disrupted by a cold front   moving in   bringing the rain
     the snow   something wet.   Yesterday I spoke to my students
about character   and conflict   desire and fear   I was meaning
what I said for once   I cared   and I wanted them to care
     and the hard part about life   friends   is that we can never really know.
Today I care about you.   The sun outside slowly disappears and over
a cheeseburger   and curly fries   we come to make   some sort of model
     of the universe   or one single universe   a universal form
          a poem in the makings.   My mother   on the phone
worried about my father   mom and dad   please call home
sometimes we can be a long ways off   from the moment   in which we were
     born.   I tell my students   a character has an arc
like a plot   You are born   you live   you die
     and in-between you might have known someone   you might have
          loved someone   been loved   been hated
been indifferent   you might have refused indifference   refused to settle

you might have bought into the American dream   regardless
bought into your own dreams   regardless   your dreams might have
         crushed you   regardless   who you were   or what
                    you wanted   they might have trembled above your head
         in the cool light of a half moon   the moon most plain
being neither full   nor slight   the moon being in-between
         and cold on a winter's night   you might have believed in yourself
         regardless   of the world   the world might have believed in you
regardless of yourself   I am reading the world   these days   for signs
and in reading I find them   but I can't say   what they mean, exactly
         or if it is wise or foolish   to let the 11:11 on the clock   the 2:22
mean something   does it mean anything   is it more   or less
do I devote myself   or how do I devote myself   to time.
         It's the time of the season.   I pour whiskey and turn on
                    another record.   You turn on   and over and we're good
         to go.   The trash truck   beeps   and backs down
the road and the dog growls   and backs down
from such a large beast.   Men in their Dickie's   the stench
         on their hands   they applaud the winter   its firm hand on the filth
                    that would rise in the summer   from maggot to adult
and take flight here   and there   and all around the dark horse's eye.
         Today   I miss the horse's eye.   I miss the sweat of summer
                    the tall grass of spring   I miss the orange of fall   I miss myself
sometimes   I miss you   I miss my mother   I miss my brother
who has died   and gone into signals   and creaks in the floor
         and windows   and signs and signs and signs   and all
the signs have pointed toward you   they have been consistent   about this
                    and sometimes in their consistency   they amaze me
bewilder me   my bewildered brain   fighting to make some meaning
         out of this living thing   the whole she-bang   the whites
                    of the eyes   and the mad dark pupils   Pupils, listen
and listen well   for a good story   will often begin in sound.
         The presidential candidates move on   through the world   and somehow
         this slowly becomes a soundtrack   to my moving   a background
         not the background I would choose   mind you   but behind me sometimes
I feel the board painted   and held up   the reflection of things
in my past   posters for future events   small screens with the faces
         of politicians   slamming each other   apologizing for slamming
each other   saying This is petty   let's stop   but as the
pettiness
         continues   finding themselves unable   not to dive back in.
And strange that this pettiness   gives me hope   insomuch as it proves
to me that these are humans   they were children once   and fought
         like children   once   with their cousins   and brothers and sisters
         fought for the bicycle   the popsicle   the teddy bear   the remote

control   the designer jeans   the cologne   the razor   the brand
      new pair of high-heel shoes.   This may not be the best quality
to have as a president   it may be the worst   but I am one human
trying to understand myself   as such   and I am understanding
      that from top to bottom   we are not so different   we are
positively different   we are mixed and matched and stretched and burned
we are cold together now but not all cold some dressed for the occasion some wearing
no coat some by the fire some by the heater some with no heat some starved some
hungry some full some full of themselves enough that it heats them to the core some
empty some dirty some dirty some definitions needed relatively to define the cold
temperature cold the cold heart the beating of that cold heart despite despite despite
as the wind picks up and spits something out   a drizzle or rain
      a cold rain turning   to snow snow turning   to a season
a settling calmness   and reservation inside   as outside the world
      does its thing   and the muffler of a large truck moans
      and moans for the tires   and moans for the man inside
and moans because for all of its traveling   for all of the mud it has only
      one song   the mad grumbling moan   the engine   turned
over
early in the morning   warming itself slowly   before it's free
to leave   or bound   to go to work   before its day has begun
      before it has any conception   of destiny at all   choice at all
before it finds itself   mirror   finds itself   taillight   finds itself
      blinker   brights   windshield   the cold wet air   today
a nice thing on its face   and my face   as I look up   and beyond
      and wonder.   Cold today.
      Cold tomorrow.   It's been cold all week
      and driving to Tulsa   the wind whipped   the car around
heading to the airport   to pick up Galway Kinnell   for a reading in Stillwater
      Don't cry   he once said   Or else, cry.   We discuss
weather when I don't know what else to say   when I have a thousand other
things to say   we rely on the familiar   and he talks about
      the temperature in New Hampshire   Vermont   the snow
and the snow   and the snow.   So I have little
      to complain about   relatively   it is very warm here
      relatively   it is exceptionally cold here   and how one handles
      the cold perhaps   says something about us as individuals
as groups of individuals   people of the map   topographies of arms and legs
      and hands and feet   and cold flesh rising and rippling across the skin.
Consider the northerner vs. the southerner   an old consideration
in which we supply   mentality   to geography
      temper   to the warm southern waters   iciness
to those living around the Great Lakes   this goes back a long way
      this goes back to people wanting only   to live   longer
better   and so forth   and moving across a continent

just so they could breathe more easily.   What a concept.
I compare men.   I compare women.   And women and men and humans
          to dogs   and on the public broadcasting channel   I recently watched
a special on dogs   and the evolution of dogs from the bloody fang
          of a wolf   into thousands of species. According to the television
          recent DNA tests suggest that all humans come from one woman
                    a great mother who lived in Africa long and long and long time ago.
On Oprah my mother and father   in different parts of the same town
          watched as a cattle farmer from one town over   was reunited
                    with a relative   the descendent of a slave
who was either raped or loved or just held for a while   by a great grandfather
of this now grandfatherly man.   It was a celebration   of sorts
          a lesson on the birthday of MLK   an illustration that we are all
not so different   that it's a small world   after all. And after all
          of this   the music plays   and after all of this we still know this
we have always known this   but sometimes as humans it is hard to remember
what we have known   what we have wanted to know   need
          to know or not   or now or never   etc.
          DNA tests reveal that dogs
          like humans   are descendents of one breed   and as that breed
spread out and adapted   the dogs changed   for instance
          in Mexico they lost their hair and were sacrificed   as holy
          to the gods   for instance   in the cold tundra
          they morphed into Huskies   pulled sleds   and fed their owners
what they could find   seal blubber   and birds   and other foods
          in that vast land   where food is scarce   they kept them
off the bad ice   kept them moving   in bad weather
          it was said   that without dogs   man in many
          parts of the world would not have survived.   I stare at my dog
sitting on the couch with me   a best friend if there can be said to be
such a thing   and rub his head   as he looks up again
          where a wolf howls on t.v.   and considers for a moment
evolution   and descent.   The dog was trained to bark instead of howl
          as a means to guard   its humans.   Funny how things change.
          Today is right now a sunny day   today is my birthday
January 24   an Aquarius   once born   now 29   one more year
and the front digit changes.   So now you know my sign
          the water bearer   and I carry water   from my home to yours
I have been carrying water all year   this year   in rain and storm
          and ice and frost and snow and the low spots of lakes   I have carried it
from the kitchen to the bedroom   the kitchen to the living room   my wet hair
          as I run late to work   in the two-thirds of my body
that persists   despite   and keeps itself from spilling over and running
          away and all through the ground.
          So the wind chill drops   and it rises   it reflects

            a different temperature   a true temperature   not scientific
but using science to determine   what the body feels versus what is real
        it is a number   set down in writing   so that we know
science does not prove everything   there is cold   and colder
there is a number   and then the way that number pushes
        against my skin   drying my lips   my hands   cracking
            them   opening them up   to the cold   and more
wind   the dry one that turns from the north   and comes around the house
        finding me in my robe   a sock hat   in the early morning
            taking the dog out once again   chilled   as it finds me
        shivering   as it finds me   whipping around the squared edge
and coming   coming hard as the full moon slowly sets.
            And where were you when the north wind turned and spake?
Inside   outside   where you hungry then   almost happy then
        were you watching the news as it mapped out a sort of geography
            of the local world around you   the international world
did you feel hopeful or lost or sad or depressed as the President addressed you
        through your television, on nearly all the channels, a suit and a mic and congress
        and the state of the Union.   And through this union, we unite.
On the high bluffs of the Mississippi River the wind spins a soul into thought
such a long way down   such a long way back   such a long time thinking
        about the long, long way of life   this river   its majesty
your highness   I bow down and with my lips kiss the cracked floor.
Do I upset you?   Do I calm you?   What fears
        underneath do we have   of each other   of one
another?   What gives?   We give the message back
        we return   and turn   and turn away
we answer   our manners   we polite   we sharp
we shake hands firmly we look you square in the eye   we want to know
        what you're made of   are you man enough   woman enough
are you just enough to save someone in disrepair.   I put a quart of oil
in the car and thank it for being there for me.   On I-35 I talk with it a short
while,
        talk with him, my car, my trusted pal   because somewhere
I believe he hears me   wants to hear me or needs to   to go on.
So I believe strange things about automobiles   and strange things
        about myself   perhaps too much   of myself
            perhaps I supply too great an importance   to a conversation
        with a car   that it can keep the motor running   motoring
        on and on and on into the long haul   the short haul there
and back   fill 'er up and you get two dollars off the car wash
        which I take   being conscious of my car being conscious of itself
madness for a machine is such a strange thing to admit.   And Kerouac
        was all for the mad people   mad to live   mad, mad
            but I am not myself always mad   or how does one define

                                                                                                85

this madness   I am lost between a madness   and an inconsideration
for madness   this is madness itself   north-northwest   the wind
the winter   now and again playing   the role of Hamlet.
And at the local diner   the dirtiest in town   I eat
with my mom and dad   dad ordering an omelet without meat   eating better
while I pour syrup over the sausage   and wonder   who will see
the first ghost.   The ghost of Christmas past   today
the ghost of Christmas future   but where the present ghost
as the ghosts occupy all three dimensions   and always the present
and perhaps only but always the present defined   by what has passed
what may come   they are calling tonight   for snow.
So now snow   and at long last I may have winter   in this a winter poem
I may be cold   it may be white   this might be
a symbol   a sign   fate or chance   or neither
but I have no answers.   In the history of my 28th and 29th years
on this the planet earth   I was aloof   at times   I was cold
at times   I was hopeful   and harmful   and harmless
I was at the local feed store   buying new shirts   I was looking forward
to the spring   looking forward   to a thousand things   looking back
at that long road on which I'd come   I was conscious
of being conscious   thirsty   some days   hungry   too
some days   some days playing the music loud with the windows down
the thermometer hitting sixty   I   hitting the steering wheel   percussion
sing along   before the song rises up in you and shatters.
Correspondences with friends across the country   a friend in France
lines cut between other friends   and the high winds   25-35 mph
cutting the lines with heavy branches coming down   in the backyard
I tear down a dead limb and walk away   throwing it on a pile
that is now a history of dead limbs   dead trees   a history I am partly
responsible for   a history that goes on before me   will go on
after me   I am historic insomuch as I am inconsequential
in the larger scheme of things   if there is a larger scheme of things
or perhaps I am everything   the scheme itself
waiting for the messages to reveal themselves.   Days ago the green began
to reveal itself   early   too early but so it goes   plants
and their nonsense   their hope   bravery   foolishness
and soon come the daffodils   along fence lines   in the yard
soon bloom and white and yellow   soon blossom   but too soon
and the world will knock them back into their coffins
too soon   and they will have to try again   but they will try again
and they will succeed again   and die again and return to this place in which
they are now again   to hope again   to wait again   to spring
upon a nice day   as a wild dog springs on wild meat
there is metaphor in their springing   and no metaphor
also life   also living   also dying   and the struggle not to

die   to survive   to complete the cycle
end the cycle   begin again the cycle that spins around   the ace of spades
flapping in the spokes of bicycle   a retro sound
a pack of cigarettes rolled in the sleeve   a day of remembrance
a day of looking onward   out the window   at the grass
still brown   still brittle   still frozen and away
but underneath   in this the winter season   a cold green coughs
and mumbles   rumbling inside the seed.
And now snow   at last
it comes   falling from the north   the winter
revealing itself   laying down a pattern
of white   a soft canvas   for the tree limbs behind
a soft canvas for the light brown back of the white-tailed doe
a white plan to start over   as it begins to fill
the spaces between   the brown grass   the green grass
opening the fridge in the early morning and pouring a cup of milk.
The weather calls   for 3-5 inches   which is either only
a dusting   or a blizzard   depending on where you come from
how you take the snow   but I am taking it as it comes
for whatever it is   right now   it is everything   I want it to be.
White   on gray   the cold
morning   and the dog   dips his nose in
sniffs   and lets loose.   This is his
first   and for me, too
sometimes   it is like seeing   again
for the first   time   the markings
of time   the wind
the accumulation   as it   drifts
an embankment   of powder.   Ashes
to ashes   dust   in the form
of water   this is where   I keep coming
back   back
back   to the winter   it has come
for me   it has announced   itself
Yea, I   Winter   keeper
of the cold   keeper   of the life
to come   keeper
of the fallen   leaves   the fallen
limbs   the fallen   trees
of the beaver   keeper   of the water
in the ice   the sleet
the slush   on the side
of the highway   the fallen   fallen down
on their knees   their backs
slowly beating   out   an image

                                          of angels.
In the other room   a clock   strikes the hour
         playing the Ave Maria   and Maria
                        wraps a scarf   around her head
today   a shawl   over her shoulders
         and lights a candle   and says a prayer
                  and looks up outside the church   as the flakes
grow larger   and decides that something
         must be answered   something   must have been
         answered   I am answering you   Maria
Maria you can find me   in the valley   wrapped tight
in a ball   my legs to my chest   my chin to my knees
         I am waiting here   to disappear   come and tuck me in
                  around bedtime.   This is a weather journal.
         A personal journal.   A diary of the sequence of me
what has been me   what is not me   the narrative I supply
         to myself   as speaker   for the white   a speaker
for the person behind this   speaker for what   that person
         hides   for what the snow now hides   and more
                  and more   throughout the day.   Beside me
a grocery list   growing longer   more expensive
         and at the store they will be low   on bread   milk
eggs   potatoes   as they are always low
         when the weather comes   and the townspeople
                  stock up   and lock down   and hold on
to each other   for what could last forever   but will likely melt
         in just a few days   it is the fear of survival
                  it is the hope   that we will have to fight
for survival   that fantasy   I hold inside   of the
end
         of the world   the end of capitalism   the end of academics
                  the end of money   debit cards   the end
of gas at the gas stations   politicians on the t.v.   the end
         of Sears   Wal-Mart   Wal-Mart taken over by the mad people
                  the starving people   the cold people come out
         of the snow   bare, hungry, and wild   to eat   to gather
to warm themselves   in the fellowship   of this large place
         under the glow   of skylights   the white on the ground
                  reflecting the white overhead   that bright darkness
         of a winter wonderland.   As I am a gambler
I'll bet   that this will not happen   even though we fear it
         or hope for it   are indifferent toward it   it will not
happen   but the possibility of it   happening
         these happenings   shape our lives   the deep places
                  in our memories   our visions of the future

tomorrow   when yes, the world is over   but it's almost
worth it   not to have to go   into work   again
          punch the time-clock at eight   again   take a morning
          smoke break   at 10:15   a thirty-minute lunch
at 12:30   an afternoon   a 5:00 drive home
a radio station   interrupting the DJ   to let everyone know
          of a weather advisory   whether or not everyone cares.
          Such a mad flurry now outside my window and I am moved by how the winter
          returns, as it has been here, always, but it comes back now, thick, down,
                    a pageant of snow flakes, the static of a television set with no darkness
                    no black, only the quiet of the white, the hush of the wind, the push
of a drift against the house, this room on the north side, this pasture out back, these
animals in the woods making preparations for a long day, and the winter, and the winter
          that ends it all, the winter that hides it all, the small hands of a child folding paper
          and clipping shapes out of the edges, unfolded into something beautiful
unfolded   into something   symmetrical   the cartography
          of a snowflake   the map   of young desire
intricate   and complex   and wholly confusing
          how ultimately   any of us ever came to be.
So come down   now   with the heaviness of winter   and I will tell
          a story   of how we fought with each other
          how we held each other   how we walked hand-in-hand
through the globe   as it shook   so small inside
          the glass looking out   so full of promise   and the soft
          wetness   of a pattern dissolving on skin.
Then the next day   and the snow melts   the temperatures
          return   to the sixties   and Oh, the sixties
          when life was different   when I was nothing
          not even a glimmer in my father's eye   or perhaps
just a glimmer then   perhaps the image of a son then
          perhaps I was already written   the story of my life
          read by some ghost in the library of neverending ghosts
          a cold finger pulling a book off the shelf   blowing the dust away
and sitting down.   I read today that NASA will send tomorrow
          a digital recording of the Beatles' "Across the Universe"   literally
across the universe   where the music will travel   the words
will travel   431 years to Polaris   the north star
          431 years to say Thank you   in one of the only ways we know
Thank you, Polaris   you have guided us for so long now.
          So, so long   John, Paul, George, and Ringo
          may you be heard   may we all be heard   our voices
our miseries   our hopes   our loves   carrying on perhaps even after
          we all are gone   431 years   where will we be
extinct   or drinking a vitamin shake   and closing the lid
          of a garbage-powered flying car   kissing the children goodbye

and off to work on the moon   to sell the stars
        galactic real-estate   a little hideaway just west of Mars.
Punxsutawney Phil walked out on Saturday and proclaimed Six more weeks
        of winter.   I have time yet to write.   The Seer
of Seers   the Prognosticator of Prognosticators   has climbed out
        of his hole   and seen   his shadow   saying
            As I look around me   a bright sky   I see
a shadow   beside me.   So it walks with Phil
        as it walks with me   what the light does to my own image
            the collection of my image on the ground   cast out
cast under   my feet   cast deep into the depths of the self
        and how that self maintains   itself   showers each morning
            combs its wind-whipped hair   brushes its teeth
and in its gray darkness   howls.   Superbowl Sunday
        in which the New York Football Giants   attempt to play spoiler
to the undefeated New England Patriots.   The hearts of men and women
        wound-up in a game   the mortgage payment bet on the spread
the over   the under   the bean dip
        delivery pizza   hot wings   ice-cold lager   drank one
            after the other   after the other   the mythological
half-time toilet flush   heard round the world.   An American holiday.
        A celebration of capitalism   commercials   television
            hooting and hollering   and the pigskin   tossed
through the air in the hopes of becoming legend.   And so the ball will fly
        and as it flies its shadow will stretch across the ground   the green turf
            at a slight angle across the field today   in Arizona
the shadow as the promise   of gravity   the other story
        of flight mapped out on earth   the story of the heavens
as they are told again   by men and women looking up   holding
        their breath   watching as it comes down gently
            into the soft hands   of a strong, fast man.
A Super Sunday   today   and later this week
        A Super Tuesday   as the candidates spread their wings
            across the states   making promises
smiling and smiling   shaking their fists   as the shadow
        of a bird crosses their face   and fights against the wind.
            The ghost of a barn   in the field out back
        and Claxton   the cattle-farming neighbor   threatens
to write a letter to the city.   On a warm day here
        we could all burn   as the weather goes dry
and the wind picks up   a day of snow   a day of wildfire   this
the kind of life we live here at times.   A slight dusting today
the day after   the presidential primaries the day after   I talked
        with a friend in Hawaii   farming there   getting ready
to harvest   and the world is such a long way away sometimes

90

so far   so vast   so easy to pick up the hand-held
and truncate time.   In the woods   to the right of my house
          an owl sits and marks the darkness   an owl as symbol
of death   I hear   I know   and so I sit and wonder
if it is I he has come for   she has come for   no known sex
to this owl   just as we never ask   really   what the Reaper
looks like under that black robe.   Today I could sneak
a peak   but sometimes in knowing you have to give up   something else
          you have to surrender the mystery   and sometimes the myth of that mystery
is much greater than the truth.   But Truth   Capital T
          All   Beauty!   and why not ask for it   why not
in this the postmodern world   the contemporary world   the world
          making up neo- and post- and pre- and new names for itself   to give
          itself an identity   forge into something new
          become something greater   something named   something more
than the winter's snow of last year   it is the ice storm of this year
          the record-setting 79 degrees just two days ago   and today, 45
snow on the ground   how in the world does the world continue
          to work.   I drink coffee   and wait outside
in my sock hat for the dog to do his business.   You are off reading
somewhere   right now   you are reading this minute
          your mind deep into a story   lost or wandering off
          into your own story   looking out
          the window   now come the birds   looking out
now come the sun   looking out   now come the man walking
          down the road and looking back at you.
                    As we close in on the end of winter the end of winter
closes in on us.   No buds on the vine   yet   no leaves on the trees
          a system of skeletons   still   today
          nature's anthem   covered
          by the hollow sound   of wind on tree limbs   a tree creaking at its fork
speaking to itself   moaning in pain   in argumentation
          to the other side where two roads diverged in a woods nearby
and I   I   I took the one…
          I have walked in a circle this morning   through the trail of the white-
          tailed deer   the small herd of doe   that come out
          each morning   each evening   in the crepuscular hours
to eat and wander and look back at me.   A forest in miniature
          a stream in miniature   a creek carrying the runoff from the snow
that now melts   carrying it back to the lake   back to the source
          of all life   spreading outward   slowly, slowly
          the great wings of water   where the lone buck dips
his antlers   and pays his respects to the howling call of Pan
          and paws the earth   and drinks.
          In the oven now my breakfast cooks.   And I am thinking

91

this morning about Galway Kinnell   alone   in a cabin   eating oatmeal
cooked on a small burner   I am thinking about him   who was thinking then
        about Keats   and oatmeal   but I am not thinking about oatmeal
                at all, but Keats now   who wrote:
            "Too happy, happy tree, / Thy branches ne'er remember /
Their green felcity:"   I am agreeing with this   I am arguing
with this   I am staring out the window   this second
        recollecting
            my own breath as it slowly escapes my body   and on and against
the window   the fog on the window   the water condensing there
            while on the other side the trees sit   and what do they remember
do they know the spring to come   do they know the abundance of mulberries
        the green of early pecans   do they sense   innately   their birth
are they born anew   each time   reincarnated every year
            as a tree set to map out   the joy   sorrow   of the house
around which they stand   the tears of a deer as the cold wind makes her eyes
        water   the water as it goes down everything as it goes down
what do the roots think   in December   what do the roots remember
    in January   it is February now   nearing the end   what does the shadow
    of a naked limb   stretched out   over the barbed wire
what does the shadow understand about time   and time to come
        where exists   once forgotten   that green felicity.
In my memory now it returns   but it is not actual   it is simulation
as I attempt to recreate   blossom   to recreate   the brook
        babbling in the sunlight   the wildflowers in bloom along its edge.
The winter releases nothing   it is held in   by the snow
        held strong by the long arms of the pines   and cedars
it is clinched in a blue berry there   dying   from the inside
        going ripe   and then dry   and then falling
to the ground to begin again.   The winter   releases nothing
            it holds tight   to what it has buried
    it clings   to what it would keep warm   to what it would
shoulder   what it would mother   what it would indifferently forget
        when it was the time to forget   what it would indifferently remember
        when it is the time to remember   this is the winter
            and the bright darkness   and the exposition
        for everything to come.   A long pause   and the reflection
rippled, rippling   in the cold water.   I take off my shoes
        my socks   I venture in calf-deep   where my ankles freeze
and I do this in reaction   to a hundred things   I crave
        to let out   let out into the cold deep   the long body of water
            stretching from cove   to outlet   to tributary
        where the beaver braves another tree.   I want something out
            of me   but even this something   is too cold to let go
        the water too cold to take it   shivering   purple and blue

not enough of a balance   too much of a balance   too much of winter
      tonight.   Where do you take   the part of you
that you can not take   anymore?   I place bets on a horse
            a thousand miles away   and today   it gives me no comfort
      the losing gives me no comfort   but the gamble itself
is still comforting   the gambling absent of the win   gambling as an
act
      of faultless hope   flawed hope   an exacta box
            and I close my eyes as they come in   not wanting to know
      just to let some horse know   some jockey   some owner
some situation   that I have invested something.   I invest nothing
      in the stock market   little into a savings account   and across town
            a woman is investing quarters   into a commercial dryer.
      Closer to home   at the Dragon's Lair   a man is investing ten dollars
for a lap dance   with some other woman   who has come
      to pride herself   on her ability to give an erection across the great expanse
            of clothing.   And on the roof the steam comes out
from the dryers   the steam comes out   from the fryers
      and off the chest of the woman dancing   in a cold, dark room
      the steam comes out and offers its own story   of water in winter
as I breathe heavily in the backyard   the steam from my own mouth
      evidence that I am still alive   such a constant surprise
            source of wonder   strangeness   as I am away from myself
while seeing that self vaporize in the air in front of me.
      A winter thunderstorm and the lightning   clings to the freezing rain.
Such strange weather this year   tornados tearing through Arkansas
      and Memphis   that city I love   and on the news
            the tin-stripped studs revealing the bones   of a restaurant
where some family came out to eat   went in   hungry   came out
      fearing for their lives   the hunger gone   the hunger
            animalistic   the hunger in the nose of a hungry dog
      dipping into something dead in the long field   savoring that foulness
            for what it is not   the comfort of a bowl and dry meal
it is not   and looking up to a bark in the distance.
      What is becoming of the world?   I look at the winter
            sometimes as a test   for what we can stand   for what
we allow ourselves to stand   to take   to grin   and bear
      even as our lips crack   and our knuckles bleed   even
            as we take it across the cheek   wet and frozen
      broke down and busted   a flat tire   and no one caring
enough to stop in the bad weather   a long night alone
      feet frozen and weary   wanting only to hum a tune   but even
too cold to hum that tune   as the melody rattles against your teeth.
      February and the future.   I ask the crystal ball   what it holds
and the crystal ball is too cold to reply   only a murky stillness   and the image

of myself as a child   wandering with my brother on my right side
      I am distant from that place   distant from the first daffodil
   distant from the slow dull pain of a sunburn in July   distant from the warm
hum of wind across wheat in September   I am winter   in a thousand
      directions   a thousand ways   I am weary
        and the dog waits at the door   wanting to take what the ground
now reveals   wanting to revel in that secrecy   I am weary
      and too cold to go out with him   go on with him   too cold
      but I bundle up and head out the door with him nonetheless
      where he bucks and lets loose in the air   and stands proud against
the coming storm   running behind me when it thunders
      I can see he trusts me   with his life   and at times this is my greatest
torment   my greatest gift   my greatest greatest as I rub his head
      and look up.   So I wait.   We wait.
      I wait with the weight of that cold water on my legs
the pressure of water   all over me   of living   all over
me
      I am winter   and other than winter   as I feel it
      all against me   living against me   breathing
against me   the great sadness   to be outside of it
      the great joy   that I am a part of it   even dying is a part of it
      the ashes in a coffee can thrown wild into the curling wind
      the story of a man in ten-thousand thousand pieces   his life set sail
to be buried on its own terms   returned on its own terms
      to the early green of late March.   And the boots march
      and we all march   one day after another.
The heavy weather vane   on the roof of an old barn   goes east
      and then south   and then spun out of control
      and then not at all.   What brings you to this place?
How have you come to find yourself here   in a graveyard
      laid out on a blanket   the day so cold behind you
      the ground so cold below   what comfort do you find
      in blankness   and laying down   if I built you a coffin now
could you sleep?   I am not sleeping   I am sleeping
      too much   the weather keeps us knocked down stuffed under the covers
      the heater hums and flares and squeaks its constant tune
      and I am grateful to be in an old house   with a gas unit in the floor
I am happy at least to have this place to find warmth.
      It will get better, they said.   And it has gotten better.
      This too shall pass, they said.   And it has passed just as one-hundred
storms have passed outside my window   just as one-thousand bolts of lightning
      have foreshadowed the thunder to come   one-Mississippi
      two-Mississippi   three-Mississippi   and thunder
      again   shaking the windows again   where we hold on
to the darkness when the darkness is all there is to hold   to each other

when we are there to hold   and the storm comes   and the storm
          passes   and the weather tells every truth I have ever known
     it hides every lie I have ever not known   it reveals everything
exposes everything   the winter places everything directly before you
     but being right before you   it is easy not to see   it is easy
          to pull your hood tight   put your face down
     spit into the ground below you, grumble, and walk on.   But I look up
because there is a story being told.   I look up because I have no right not to.
     I am as guilty as the next. I am as human as the next.   I am faulty
          broken sometimes   I am not used to people being either too kind
or too angry   too exceptional   or too away
     I am on the mission this winter, this February, this 11th day of the month to know
someone, hold someone, believe in someone even knowing what belies, that fate belies, even
believing that fate tells all, holds all, I am staring up to the stars in their constant silver, looking
older in the winter, colder in the winter, even though they are galaxies away, burning
themselves up so that they might be seen, on some nights, on others not, in the sky, beside the
moon   as it travels   in its strange half-circle across this sky
     to a world beyond of horizons and rivers and people waiting for the night.
          Morning   and my mother says   it is always coldest
the moment before   the sun rises   that the temperature drops
     as if the ground is holding on   tighter   to what it has become
in the night   holding on tighter   until it lets it go
     gives it up   and opens its broad face to the morning light.
          So morning has broken   because it does break
it breaks with the past   it breaks with the day before   the future broken
     like an egg   dropped into hot butter and oil   fried in a pan and served
     with toast.   Today is Valentine's Day   a signal
for the spring to come   for love to come   a name referring
     to several saints   a shady holiday   as if the saint himself
          rests in the shadows   breathing hard   petting the thigh
of some woman against the church wall.   It is a day
to proclaim love.   I love you.
          Easy as they come or difficult as they come
          love them as they are   and each other as we are   I love you
for everything you are and are not   for your face from a distance
     your face right before me   your back   your arms   your legs
          the sharpest parts of your soul.   Good morning
and this day presents at last the hidden message of winter
     the one that was held all along   held for so long   in secrecy
in darkness   in the twisted gut of a sixteen year old drinking enough beer so that
     today   he will get this off his chest   it has been held
          by the young school children   who know little about love
as we define love   who know everything about love   as love
has no definition   they bring their cards today   their Be Mines
     their Kiss Me   they spread their colored hearts across their desks

and offer the heart as message   the heart as poem   the heart
          as simple, sweet and saying the only thing it knows to
                    the only thing it wants to   clearly and without reservation
I love you   forever   and ever.
          Forever such a long word   but a word the winter knows
well   a word which holds within it   promises of the flesh
          promises of the mind   promises of the soul   if you believe
               in souls   and today I do.   We sat and discussed
magic realism   and I said that ultimately   it comes down
          to what a person decides to do with the ghosts that they see
                    the visions they see   the unknown shadows walking
          through the woods late at night   bared by the winter's ribs
cracking through the dry wood   not a deer nor a man nor a beast nor anything
          easily understood   something in that darkness that even
               scares the owl who sometimes scares me   or perhaps
          the owl fears nothing, knowing   that in those woods
a soul passes through   something long and old and loved
          for a long, long time   and thought about by the living
sometimes   sometimes, remembered   and wept over
     spilt over   thought about as I take a quarter
          from my pocket at a local bar and play "Sister Christian"
          and order a whiskey   and close my eyes   where inside
something else sings   not someone else   but another there
          an away that is away from me   and always a part of me
and when I say I am cold   it is the part that recognizes another cold.
          And when I say that I am thirsty   it has an entirely different thirst
               that need be quenched.   And when I say I am tired.
          And when I say I am weary.   And when I say I am old
and lost   and moved   and emotional
          and when I am myself more than I can understand   different than I
can understand   changed and changed and changing
                         then I look out the window at the last of this winter
          one winter   held fast   and strange
and bitter and strong as all winters are   one winter
          vicious with its people   its plants   its own soul
               tethered between the frozen days   the thawed days
          one winter in constant confusion   but constantly burying
the fall   constantly burying   the summer
          the spring of before   the work of before   one winter
as the farthest thing from the year itself   the season away
          the flower away   the birds singing in the early light this morning
for food   singing their weary blues   singing for love
          the love to come in the spring   singing for a future image
               of their selves   their selves as they currently reside
          two to a tree   three on the line   in the backyard

and coming down now and again for food.
   with the winter today
     its unapologetic face
for what it does may seem cold
   dishonest
     may seem greedy
   to know what the winter knows.
on this the day of love
   I love you for what you hold underneath
     what is cold
when you bare yourself   to me.
   you hide beneath your light skin
     that has fallen there
   both the seeds that have died
and the seeds that have lied dormant
   and now with the winter
     and turn upward to the sun
   through the dirt   but it is warm there
and they know it less for the miseries
   less for the miseries it has at times held
     more   for the promise
   sealed in their envelopes   their letters
now read   as they slowly begin

   I am filled
its wholeness   its absence
   for what it does
   for what it hides may seem
for what it keeps as its winter secret
when all around we need
   When I say I love you, today
I mean that I love you like I love the winter.
   for what is buried
what is singular
I love you for the green splendor
   and every leaf
every seed   that earth has buried
   in the early hours of a killing frost
quiet   and waiting
let go   and open up
   not seen yet
   and pleasant
it will hold at times
in winter   they know it
   that they have
   now open
   the story of vernal life.

IV. & RETURN

On Easter morning the first buds burst into green
on the limbs of the old tree beside the house,
speckled there like the first freckles on the early sunned back
of this woman beside me in a white tank top,
white on green, life on right, I pull a shirt over my head
and head out into the morning sun as it cuts through the windows
on the east side of the house, east and west, a canopy of brightness the sun pulls down
over the world, and the daffodils come, the purple clover pushes up and takes over
the yard, the wind pushes the first small leaves of the spinach in the garden,
it has begun, the beginning, it is starting all over again.
Spring break this past week on campus, and we are all breaking open.
We are coming out of our shells, cracked like the egg going into some meringue,
the whites carefully separated from the yolks, whisked into a cloud of sweetness.
The egg as Easter symbol, and symbols, what a thing to think of, how not to—
to live today is itself, for me, a symbolic act.
St. Patrick's day just a week gone,
the green beer brought out in cold glasses, taken down, so that we put back
into our bodies what has been missing so long,
we put back the earth there, we put back the skies there, the sun there,
the there of a night on the town, a celebration for things to come,
a hotel bar and black leather seats, karaoke sung by the old and young, sung well,
here, tonight, sung sincerely, the real world revealing itself,
as even on the arm of the weathered waitress, the mountains tattooed there
flower and open up around the base, the ink revising itself.
A landscape. A cityscape. A hope that escapes the chest, out through the mouth,
breathed there, deeply there, in front of me so that I can see it as one sees the future,
the fortune, the past of the right-palm, what's left to come on the left,
the palm fronds waived in churches on a Sunday morning, we are the hush, we are the push,
we are the breeze bringing in the rain.
In another booth an old man in thick glasses goes slowly through the song list,
never singing, never signing on, but holding on to the thought of singing,
of finding the right song, a song for a woman, a song to dance to, and we dance,
without caring about getting the steps right, alone on a pale blue floor.
Returning from the restroom I see the same man,
beckoning a young girl to practice with him there in the fluorescent light,
where things mean less, and in meaning less, more, as she replies,
I'm sorry but I don't know how to promenade. The spring promenade begins outside
in the darkness, the parade of floral color, local color, the people head out into the streets
and walk, with the dog, with the neighbor, hand in hand with a new love.
Rte. 66 and Anne's Chicken House, classic rock on the radio, fried peaches,
a burger big enough it intimidates even me. I am not always so easily intimidated.

101

I am sometimes scared to death. Or not death, but to life,
we are going in another direction now, we are pulling up the weeds of winter, the thick plugs
of Bermuda that pop up here and there in the garden, pulling up a French fry,
pulling up a cold coke, a book off the table, a story that begins
with two people signing their names on a restaurant wall.
In Missouri and Illinois the rain comes and floods the Mississippi, as it crests today,
perhaps even as I write, swelling with a message from the north, the tributaries,
the thousand little towns, the thousand houses, the thousand homes
and people within those homes, planting things, their hands in the soil, and it feels so good
even as the ground still holds on to a bit of cold. I have sat, this early spring, for an hour,
at least, just willing myself to see an early seedling grow.
It happens so slowly, so suddenly, too, that it's strange I can't mark it against something,
draw a line against the doorframe of the horizon, and another, and another,
as I feel responsible and proud even of such a small thing as it makes its brave entry
into the world. I have much to tell you, youngster. There is heartache,
pain, human misery and hatred, there is much here in this place not to like.
But it is so much beyond that, too, so full of potential, as when you were a young seed
you were little more than a small weight to be carried on the back of an ant, swallowed
unknowingly by a bird, you were nothing, really, without water, but everything,
you were a metaphor for you very own self.
In this fashion you were no metaphor at all, but the thing itself,
rightness itself, spring itself
as within your small black pod you held a cosmos, a world,
a tiny globe cracked open so that at last the people can see there is no hell under there,
nothing burning, no flames, no beast with a forkéd tongue,
only heat as you took it in from the sun, with the cold water, and made it a story
of your own, a story told so many times it should be old by now,
and perhaps it is old by now, perhaps I am foolish to repeat it, rephrase it, return to it
as something majestic, something impossible, something the robin shies away from
as she carefully takes the worm.
March 20th and a season officially begins. This is before Easter, even,
I am not chronological, I am scattered, held together like everything that has fallen
from the trees, taken under, brought back, I am early and I bloom, bloom, bloom.
A full moon, and as it shines through the window I lie awake,
unable to sleep, unable not to stare at the silver face and ask it what it asks,
how the face, is that a smile, you seem happy, tonight, to see me.
We go around the house quietly for each other
and hide the eggs. We hide them in the obvious places, in the strange places,
in the pots and pans hanging from the kitchen ceiling.
It is so good to find something so important.
So right. Such the feeling to represent in the smallness of rooms the grandness
of the world outside, as again, on this Tuesday, I find
exactly what I am looking for, that certain blossoming tree on the edge of the park,
that certain emotion in my heart I'd come to forget was there.
You may forget a million things, but the important ones will find you again.

The spring will find you again, if it hasn't already, dear reader,
if you are not, in this moment, on the brink of welling over.
The bucket dips into the well and with a leprechaun out comes a pot of gold.
The gold buds have now gone green. The green buds are now going
to put on a show. So promenade, and hold your partner
by the hand, or more tightly, or so tightly the two of you become little more
than one, the same story, a strange mass leaning in on itself, like two seeds
planted so closely they eventually take on each other's roots, each other's space,
each other's sunlight and swirl into one.
Friday afternoon and I spend it at the Western Veterinary Hospital.
The dog has heartworms, and so, young as he is,
he carries the history of another season in his veins, another year, another life,
another place spent cooped up in chain-link, another mosquito,
even as the mosquitoes just now begin their long and slow rise out of the wetter places
in the world, the hotter places, the swampy story of darkness.
Such a strange thing to think of: a tender heart
slowly devoured by parasites,
as they wrap their way around and through the ventricles.
We are all fighting for our lives,
and it is a good time to do so, being strong, being hopeful, being moved
by the thousand things coming up in the world,
by the fight that is all around.
A dogwood blossoms and a young girl stands on her tippy-toes
with a camera to record the bloom. This is record making.
This is recording. This is spring music as it is taken down digitally, through analog,
carved into the black reflection of a vinyl surface.
In Perkins, OK, my waitress wipes the vinyl tablecloth,
I order bbq and fry-bread, I smear the butter, I dip the bread into the honey,
such a sweet thing, wet with grease, and just what my arteries were asking for
that day. An hour later I'm at a Pawnee casino, playing roulette
on a computer simulation game, a giant television with a dealer spinning the wheel,
dropping the ball, I'm all alone waiting for my number to come in.
And all around, these screens, with smiling men or buxom women dealing blackjack,
three-card poker, other card games, and I wonder for a while
where all the real people have gone. Long time passing, and I win and then I lose
and then overall I break even, and head back out into the world,
out of the glitter and bells and buzzers and lights and smell of ground beef
constantly hitting a griddle.
You get hungry investing so much,
hungry hoping so deeply, wanting so deeply, needing so deeply.
In the deep caverns of a porcelain sink I wash my hands, my face, I brush my hair
and feel like another newer version of myself on the 29th of March.
Later that night I will fix myself a steak, and even one for the dog, not a last supper
but a last supper before he goes in for treatments on Monday.
Monday, Monday. Another week begins.

Outside my window there's a rock wall I built out of an old foundation that was piled up
in the yard. It saddens me, sometimes, that I don't know for what that foundation stood.
It also gives me the freedom to choose. Today I choose a small shack,
a one-room place with a wood heater and stove.
Look at how sentimental I can be.
In order to stack the concrete blocks I had to spend hours
breaking up the rebar, twisting it back and forth until it became warm, and then hot,
and then too energized to hold itself together any more. Even iron is fragile
under the right circumstances.
Houses. Homes. A living room and reruns of Rosanne, a couch watching a couch,
and the viewer might feel for one brief moment the sadness
of two sad worlds colliding, the void, humming there like static beside the screen,
and then some situational comedy and audience laughter and applause
and nothing was perhaps so serious as we thought.
Rain this morning. And at one of the local bars
an older woman unplugs the jukebox, not for fear of lightning but just to hear
the water as it patters on the tin roof, as she stacks the chairs, sweeps the floors,
wipes all the dirty world down with a wet rag.
Through the rain the geese fly over, honking in their ridiculous spring fashion,
there is no stopping them now, they feel it in their bones,
and the hollows of the nests they build, the children they bring forth,
the tiny goslings swimming in a row behind mother,
young fluffy potential, watch them as they learn so much.
We build a fire beside the water and all night they chatter, the insomniac geese,
there is too much going on right now to sleep.
The Bradford pears go white and speckled and reveal their subtle stench,
something sultry in that smell, sexual, visceral, that lures me in
to take a sniff, and another, even though the smell is not one that I particularly care for.
In St. Louis at a mega-store my mother meets a man in a wheelchair,
telling her of his own recently departed mother
who lived through the depression,
telling of all the money they'd been finding throughout her house,
tucked inside books, frozen in ice-trays, hidden in the mattress of her bed.
And in the attic he said they found over forty guns—
rifles, pistols, revolvers, a multitude,
an arsenal just waiting for the end of the world to come.
We drive out to the lake, down a country road and on the side there
is a wooden rocking chair,
turned over in a ditch. The arms are busted and part of the seat
is broken, but we stand it up anyway, and being thankful for being stood up,
it rocks in the wind, back and forth, glad to be rocking on such a warm day.
Everything has a story. And everyone, too.
On the local news they throw a dart on a map, find a small town,
go through a phonebook and call someone up at random.
And they have a story to tell. A lovely, honest, heartbreaking story about their children

and losing their children or a circus or winning the first state lottery
or building rocking chairs or once meeting president Jimmy Carter,
and I tell you that I think this would be a fine way to go about writing a book.
So the book never ends, but it always begins.
There is always a story, and this is mine, or part of it,
or ours, something we share, like a pitcher of beer or the same slant of sunlight,
the rain, today, as it wets our dried-out skin.
As the days progress into seventy degrees the birds
mark their return, their business.
The hawks come back. And out back, in the fields behind the house,
two turkey vultures make passing circles on some days,
on other days, only one,
but the vulture is a constant around here lately, and so I wonder,
what does this mean, is it an omen, good or bad,
life or death, am I dying?
One day I watch the lone vulture swooping through the air,
I watch it circle there against the backdrop of blue skies and small white clouds,
of circling Cessnas and other airplanes,
I watch it in the sky and then I watch the giant shadow it makes
across the ground, passing across my face, I watch
and wonder what it means to have been touched by this slight of darkness.
An acre or two over I see as the bird makes its way into the top
of a tree, and so perhaps a nest, perhaps a home.
Mowers mow. Weed eaters eat. The lawns take on our perceptions of beauty.
I spray the grass to kill the dandelions and talk to the old neighbor-woman,
Mabel, about yards and other neighbors and the nice weather.
Down the street children ride their bikes today,
and take turns shouting, whooping, hollering into that wild void of childhood.
Your horoscope for today: remember your inner child.
Sometimes I amuse children—I can't help it.
Sometimes I terrify children—
I can't help it.
But we are childlike in the mornings when the sun comes through the glass,
the prism, as the light refracts and bends its way around
the room, making a rainbow,
a promise of the color scale and passing time,
brightness bended on one knee,
holding its hand out, begging for love, to be taken in
to the sweet and strong arms of a woman who, today, cares so, so much.
Across the country in Nashville my father is in surgery this very moment,
a robotic bypass, so that two robot arms make their way
through either side of his chest, carrying out the doctor's orders prescribed
on a giant computer screen. He can keep his chest closed this way,
which I think is what he most wants. So as not to open
what hides there, what is beautiful there, what he keeps there under the ribs

and the sternum, what beats, what beats, what beats.
Also in Nashville at this very moment some woman is biting
into a hot, hot piece of Prince's Hot Fried Chicken,
a long story of wayward men and a mound of pepper, a sneeze
and revenge somehow came out tasting wrong, or right,
spicy and served every day.
At the small lake a mile or so away the turtles have returned,
they sun themselves on the logs all day,
they plop in the water slowly, they ripple, they wade with their heads again
just above water.
In a dream you said I came to you like that: up from the depths,
my face clear through the glass surface, my eyes open, surfacing and smiling
with a rented horse right behind me. I could go for a ride today.
It is a good day for that. They're calling for thunderstorms
this afternoon, every afternoon in fact it seems forever,
it is tornado season and the weathermen wait anxiously.
And a first one touches down in Little Rock, AR.
They begin to touch down in southern Oklahoma, just south of the city,
in the small towns that take pride in their small homes and small trees,
the smallness representing the wisdom of the little pig,
keeping out the weather of another year and another year,
keeping the dog in the yard chained to a tree, to bark and bark at the big bad wolf.
The light through the window is trapped
before it can blossom, or rather it is trapped in blossom, it is blooming
on the dirty white wall.
As the light returns, so does life.
In the backyard I look at the small tree, the dead one, and decide to cut it down
with a skillsaw. I saw all afternoon, thinking a dead tree
is not good karma for a backyard, or any yard,
it has been dead for almost two years and I finally had enough,
or wanted it gone enough, or needed it gone, or something to do,
you leave me all alone on a Saturday and this is what you get.
For lunch, bbq at the Elk's Blaze-a-thon. I am supporting charity
and my own hunger. I am salivating over good brisket and the Lady Elk's bake sale.
In the parking lot giant trailers and smokers line the asphalt,
with their fantastic names: O-So-Slo BBQ, Between the Buns BBQ, the sweet smoky smell
of pecan and hickory constantly burning.
Across from the tint shop another shaved ice shack opens up,
and the high school students line up after school for some tropical flavor
that beckons them to Panama City or South Padre Island
or just beckons them into something sweet and the hand of some cute boy or girl.
Their emotions sit in their stomachs like the first flames of small fires,
flaring up when the wind picks up,
they come to this place and pay two dollars to try
and put them out, or keep them going, or just to unwind from another boring day

of school. J & D Produce reopens, and I'm happy to have the first
of what will be another season of good fruits and vegetables,
jalapeños and avocados coming in right now,
white onions as big as a big baby's head.
A long hike and on the trail a group of six milk cows,
and the dog takes out after them, cow-chasing inherent to his breed, to his type,
he has found something deep inside that he is supposed to do, even though
he doesn't know why, he has heard in his bones a small man
in a cowboy hat shouting: Sick 'em.
A season of festivals. Couch Park and the Arts & Heritage exhibit, the return
of carnival food. Corndogs and funnel cakes. Lemonade squeezed out
from a stainless steel press—hard work and a sweet payoff,
this is what we come to the spring to learn.
On stage, various acts.
Tribal dances by some of the local Native American tribes, as a middle-aged man
in braids and variations of canary yellow dances through three hoops
he twists about his body, while in the distance, on the grass,
his young son dances along, knowing the steps, mimicking the turns of his father,
the beat of a drum played out on compact disk over loud speakers.
We honor the past and in doing so make little of the past.
While the dance continues, several men dressed in Union uniforms fire blank muskets
into the creekbed.
Reload. Aim. Fire.
The simulation means nothing anymore.
After the dancing finishes an old cowboy comes up, alone, with his guitar,
and picks and sings a handful of those sad and glorious songs,
and it is good to hear the music coming from its source.
Life all around comes from its source now.
I listen in as an older woman talks to a young wood sculptor about his choice
of wood, the knotty, gnarled, trash-pile he carves and sands
into something beautiful, and almost tragic in its beauty.
Tents and teepees, and nobody seems to know the difference.
Perhaps this is a good thing.
The garden continues and with the first frost coming I take out old sheets
and cover it in the middle of the night, a little buzzed from beers
at one of the local Mexican restaurants, I cover the pepper plants,
the spinach, the herbs, the tomatoes, I wish them well
and tell them I'll see you in the morning.
Morning and mourning. Wonder and wander.
The homonyms never get old, sometimes.
But they grow like the plants, they push up, out, under, go to seed,
and once they fall back into the ground they go on again, and come up again,
as they return all over even now.
Life shouldn't be this surprising anymore.
It amazes me each day.

Around campus the students begin their slow withdrawal from heavy clothing
and move into their bodies, wearing tank tops and shorts
even before the weather is ready—they have waited too long to show themselves off
to care about the cold or the light rain or the wind.
The wind comes heavy in Oklahoma.
It moves right through my chest sometimes, cuts across and through and around
my heart, whipping my hair, pruning the old branches from the trees,
it comes as the work of a gardener's hand for the big plants,
knocking down the smaller ones. Sometimes it is good to understand smallness,
relatively. The tanning salons across town bustle.
The people are preparing their skins with light bulbs for the real sun to come,
the warmth to come, and then heat, and then hotness that blurs the distance.
The preparation is an excuse, of course.
So many preparations as excuses, as we all prepare, each day, for death,
and thus the ultimate excuse to live life as if we are something alive.
The impulse to go on staying alive and the impulse to live while living.
Vice and versa. The cowboy's refrain:
You know you're gonna miss me when I'm gone.
The spring football scrimmages go on all over, where the colors play each other,
the light versus the darkness of the same team, the same self, the same body
crashing against its own shadows. In the neighbor's window pane,
through the shadows of the leaves there, in the light that breaks through,
I see the face of my brother. My mother tells me the veil
between this world and the next, she thinks, is no thicker than a thin piece of glass.
You turn off the lights, and shut down the mirror.
We hold each other when it gets cold, and tonight, it is cold again.
We are all over.
We are needles on the map.
We are phone numbers,
street names,
signatures on a license,
social security cards.
Eight hours away my friend Thrower is living right now
off Vodka and rice, writing songs and poems as we write each other, sometimes.
The first heavy spring rain comes.
In my heart, I tell myself it will bring flowers, I repeat the words.
But I worry about the flowers already come, and the garden just poking up, and the gray
blanket that seeds itself in your soul, sometimes, so that the weather
inconsistently maps out our emotions on the Doppler radar.
The waters come. It floods, and the floods recede,
leaving in their wake old chip bags and beer cans and mud gone hard covering the sidewalks,
leaving a story of where the water traveled, and how hard, and how slowly and softly
it all went down. My father returns from Nashville, and recovers well.
All of us children, and my mother, we hang on to his heart like the face
of a rock cliff. Springtime, and he blooms, too.

I read Blake, "To Spring," and think of what a man might know
about one world versus the other, the past versus the future, the hope:
"O thou with dewy locks, who lookest down
Through the clear windows of the morning, turn
Thine angel eyes upon our western isle,
Which in full choir hails thy approach, O Spring!"
The ghosts of everything I miss rise up with the purple clover,
in the rain, in the sunlight, in the shadows.
In northern Viet Nam today they discover a rare, giant turtle,
a legend of myth returned, come out to sun himself, as he rolls over and begins the universe
again. At the lake a few blocks away, the turtles return, and begin the long process
of baking themselves on the logs, thawing out to the world as it warms up
one day at a time, sweet Jesus, even while the cross-country runners go by,
and they splash back into the depths because of some instinctual fear of sound.
The thunder scares the dog, and at nights he tucks his head under my arm.
I know he doesn't know
whether or not I can protect him from the wild world and wind whipping
outside, I know he doesn't know whether I can raise one hand
and stop the rain.
But he puts some faith in me that I will try, or that I am better suited for the job
than him. And so I go on pretending that everything is alright,
and pat his head, and tell him I won't let anything happen.
There is something truly aweful about a spring storm approaching,
so wonderful, as the sky goes a dark gray green, and the wind swirls, and the first
heavy drops of rain come pounding the earth. The storm walks with a heavy foot,
and I walk out into it, and breathe in, deeply, and smell
the blend of all the life around me as it opens up,
and tilts its head back, knowing that even if it's violent and cruel
sometimes, at least it will, for a moment, quench their thirst.
An oriole sings out, and along a barbed-wire fence two mockingbirds
map out their own fence, dancing their hop along the line there, marking out a homeland
for the year to come.
Nature, and it's a spring fling.
Everybody wants someone to love,
one of their own, one they can claim, one that fills whatever space it is
that god has cut out and emptied from their souls,
a heart shape, the shape of a woman's body, the shape of a leaf
as it rises from the bud, and breaks out and open into the bright sunlight.
The sun comes out, and the earth heats up.
We go to a Latin festival and learn the meringue, a few simple steps,
and I spend some time throwing a Frisbee to another man's dog,
talking about cattle farming in New Zealand, the weather in Idaho,
he has been to some places and I have been to some places
and we have seen some things
and been through our share of hard times

and so we huddle for an hour on an afternoon and discuss.
Classical guitar music echoes over huge speakers,
but there is nothing classical about the music choice—crowd pleasers and heart breakers,
just what the doctor ordered.
We sip mojitos out of a thermos until we are as baked inside as our skin
on the outside. A piano in a cafeteria, and you play a song for me.
You are the song itself, a little song, a sonnet,
a symphony that echoes throughout each of my days.
The cool bed of an early morning, but in my head I hear Robert Herrick saying:
"Get up, get up for shame!" That girl Corinna
has gone a-Maying again," and it is soon to be May in these parts,
in this century, this decade, this year, all around this man,
the May thing that happens
when the fertilizer takes hold and the heat picks up and two neighbors
will curse each other over a pile of dirt one has had delivered, which bleeds
onto the other's property from all the hard rains.
It's just that, he wants a nice yard.
It's just that, he's a shit sometimes.
It's just that, the heat,
the slow frustration built up inside,
it's just that the world is coming out and so this anger must, too,
it must release itself in front of the whole neighborhood,
almost like a play, right there, beside the street,
in the mid-afternoon of another Wednesday.
At the high school and the university the end is near,
or rather the beginning, the both,
and at the local restaurants students will soon fill-up the booths and tables
dressed in their formal wear for prom, that night
of all nights, that anthem, that sweet build-up,
that letdown for a lifetime to come.
Or else a kiss, and a woman, and the backseat of a father's car.
Or else a child and a long and loving and lovely life together.
Who is to say what is right or wrong, young or old,
love or no, who's to say.
In myself there is a part of me that wants to know
everything so badly, all the past, all the present, all the future,
even those darkest things that would make my heart shake itself into contraction,
it wants to know. But the older I get the more
this other part of me wants only for that part of me to go away,
it wants to have never needed to know, to not need to know,
to not want to, not desire to, not fill out a narrative of terror.
So when I push a seed into the ground, I work to bury this feeling.
When the rains come down all afternoon, I walk out into the water in the hopes
of it washing away. I want to cleanse myself,
of all the terrible things I have done, to be forgiven

for what is, perhaps, unforgivable, to not need to be forgiven, to move on,
to live as the grass lives, brown one day, bright green the next,
filling out the yard just two days after I've mowed.
I mow the lawn with patience and let the hum of the motor
take over me, drown my thoughts down into deeper thoughts,
I feel the grass as it is cut, the stick as it is mulched, the rock as I run over it
just for the sparks. Sparks, and a fire ignites.
I spend ten minutes at the feed store looking at spark-plugs for the mower,
not needing one, but wanting to need one, just wanting to do something
so badly, some work, a little fix-er-upper, a something to fill
the quiet parts of my day.
In the quiet parts, sometimes, the roar of memory, like thunder,
a storm passing through my mind, of past events actual,
past events hypothesized, the great realm of the future
hovering before me like some giant man on a chair blowing cigarette smoke in my face,
and he is blurry behind it, and smiling and toothy,
and I cannot tell if he is happy for me or grinning in a sinister fashion
at my future misfortune, I cannot tell where I am going, my friends.
The turkey vulture passes over again, and I cannot explain to you, right now,
how green the world is outside my windows.
It is damp, opened up, I cannot, I cannot
explain. But in offering no explanation
you might come to need no explanation—only the quiet,
only the bird singing, the small frogs chirping,
the sun as it breaks through the clouds
and lifts our faces up.
Our faces up and they float away like balloons.
The hand of a child letting go, and they sail off together
past the birthday cake and dog barking at something moving
on the other side of the fence.
The roses call out, their subtle scent, they make something wonderful
of the Wal-Mart parking lot, or something better,
they fill up a small corner of concrete with color—
right beside a tiny little wooden home for children.
A treehouse.
We climb up into the limbs and hide away.
Spring is not the season for hiding away,
but it keeps things to itself, it begins the long and slow growth
toward summer, toward apparel, as on the limbs of the trees the leaves
do the opposite of what the men and women around here do,
a little less clothing each day until the dog days of summer return
and they are wearing little more than a small strand of the idea of clothing.
The tailpipes stop smoking in the mornings.
The blinkers hit the sunlight and as it is light on light, they meld
into one another.

I say a prayer, today, for the garden.
I say a prayer, today, for us.
I say a prayer, today, for love,
for the spring, for the shadow that I see stretching out around the corner.
On a cold and rainy night, a movie.
On a warm day, a walk.
We fill up the days
with small events and large events, we fill up the days
with each other as much as we can.
And cummings, saying in my head today
"Spring is like a perhaps hand
...
changing everything carefully."
And it is careful, and I am,
and it is not, either, because there is nothing careful about change,
I think, sometimes,
sometimes, I think
otherwise, sometimes I just don't know.
Driving to Lawton, OK, for a reading yesterday
on I-35 I passed a propeller, one prop, behind a semi, on a flatbed,
larger than I could comprehend a propeller to be,
and for a moment I couldn't figure out what it was.
Perhaps it was for a windmill,
south of Oklahoma city, where in a field beside the road
the wind turns the faces and the faces turn the power
and even Don Quixote would have turned tail
and ran. The cars run by.
The sun bakes the earth, and on some days after a hard rain
the surface cracks open.
If you look down you can sometimes see the sweltering core,
or the rotten core, or the seeds there,
whatever it is you believe to be underneath, minus science,
minus fiction, whatever you know to be true in your heart.
When it is hungry the gut can be a terrible thing,
calling out in public,
making a spectacle of the physicality of your body.
When it is paranoid the gut can be a terrible thing,
when it knows what it doesn't want to know,
when it doesn't know whether it is itself at that moment, or the head,
the brain ground into a colorful meat combination,
head cheese smeared on toasted rye.
At the Tumbleweed bar less than two miles from my house
they held, this weekend, the world's largest calf fry, the Testicle Festival,
at which they serve cold beer and live music and great heaping portions
of fried calf testicles.

What was once starvation or a dare
has become a custom here, a tradition to bring the kids to,
to get a babysitter for,
to go out all night for with your tight jeans on
in the cool breeze of a low spring dusk.
The trees outside move differently now,
they shake more fully, sashay, voluptuous with their leaves,
there is more of them to catch the wind,
more of them to dance, more reason to, with the weather,
just as the people move their bodies a little bit more each day,
and even an old man who has sworn off dancing for his entire life,
sworn off loving, sworn off the bottle, sworn off so much, even he,
with a plate of meatballs and cheese cubes
at a wedding reception,
finds himself tapping his foot to the beat.
It started: We are gathered here today…
and you asked me if this began
a wedding or a funeral.
I said both,
meaning both and both
and We are gathered here today
to take what comes at us, all of it, the beauty and the hard parts
and the pain and the love and the dog crawling up
between us.
This weekend marks the 134th Kentucky Derby,
where I will drive south
and place bets on the beautiful three year olds: Big Brown and Eight Belles
and all the others.
It is the best time to gamble, the warm weather, a cold mint julep,
the tradition, the horses, the unknown, the longshot.
The spring fills the event out, perhaps the greenest
sporting event in America, alive as America is alive,
from top to bottom, rich to poor,
the uppities and the itty-bitties
and the beautiful hats and the cowboy hats
and the ball caps and golf visors
all mapping out on our heads some idea
about who we think we are underneath, as on the dogwood blossom
you sense the kindness of that tree,
as on the locust thorn you sense a long tradition of blood.
Spring rain this morning, and today I am glad of it, at least.
The garden grows.
On my desk a winning ticket stub
for the Derby, an exacta, half of the win belonging
to Eight Belles who was euthanized just past the finish line.

I have asked myself if that's not the best way to go out—
young and full of drive and doing what you were born to do,
bred to do, a filly running hard amongst the big boys,
pushing herself, pushing the conception others have about her.
It is clean outside now,
and in Louisville the track has been washed out many times over,
the dirt smoothed by big John Deere tractors.
I feel closer to you today, we are getting somewhere,
moving toward each other,
as a year comes around and bends itself together
so too do we, face-to-face, back-to-back, always.
In Tulsa, OK, 15th/Cherry St., outside the Full Moon Café
we sit and have drinks as the first May wind pushes through,
and on the television sports broadcasting, and beside us
men discuss what is, exactly, the problem with Hillary Clinton,
what is the problem with corporate food,
the problem, the problem, the problem.
And we all have problems, but today we don't discuss them,
we raise them up between us, nestled on a board
we both carry on our shoulders, the weight of our heaviness held
between us, shared, I put it on the mantle and lay you down.
It is warm enough that even through the night the birds chirp.
Last night it was so bright, though, that the crickets
refused to make a sound, refused to risk music,
except for those that did, that sang out anyway,
under a rock or in the small parts of the world
where the world holds itself safe, and tiny, and away and dark
and quiet and quite beautiful.
The neighbors' white cat waits in the tall grass for a bird.
The dog chases all the bugs, one at a time,
through the field out back.
It can be an innocent game, I think, cat and mouse,
it can be vicious, it can be deadly, it can be the friendliest thing
an animal might ever know.
First the conditions must be right.
Secondly the animal must be right.
Thirdly the desire must be right,
the night must be right, the smell, the moon, the food the drinks
the conversation.
Still the rain comes down and a fog lifts up from the earth.
Your lips reach up to mine, mine down to yours,
I witness the heat right now hold itself together,
hold itself upright, hold itself as something held, something loved,
something needed on the seventh day of May.
Wednesday, and tomorrow the road.

A trip into what the spider knows,
what the mockingbird knows,
what the frogs swell themselves with and know, too.
The future begins like that.
It was there and then it is here.
And we walk into it, hand-in-hand,
wet today, the water running off itself, splendid and quenching that eternal thirst for life.
School lets out, and with nowhere else to go,
home, the highway, Branson, MO and a Quality Inn next to the theater
of Shoji Tabuchi. Such a strange little hideaway
in the middle of the Ozarks,
the middle of everything, really, the middle compass of America
and the bible belt and music and mirth and a generation recreated that is long gone
everywhere else.
Downtown the fudge shops and a giant Hilton right on the lake's water,
a fountain and fire show,
children and adults and the elderly everywhere,
an outdoor mall, the spring air, and we sit on a patio and drink Guinness
with French fries and curry.
Our first vacation, perhaps. Our first time to Branson,
our first time giving in to the randomness of a little dip off I-44,
first time heading south from Springfield, first time
watching the dueling pianos as the members of a sales conference sing along,
and the night wears itself into raunchiness, a bachelor's party,
and even the piano has been drinking.
The next day and the pool and the hot tub, a conversation
with my father about the goat market,
the high price of goats, and a pecan orchard where he hopes to put some up.
Springtime and the big locust trees blossom,
their sweet smell, ringing in the heart of the season with honey,
the honey that drips from the suckle now, and down
into the ground, down into the honey dew,
turned and turned in ice to make the honey ice cream,
which I buy with almonds in a waffle cone.
And the small black woman in Mississippi says this is the time
when the devil comes out, the warmer days,
the porch days, the devil in the people because the people come out to talk about the people,
they come out from their solitude, from minding their own business,
they come out into the light,
they come out into the darkness of night,
they come out into the street and sidewalks and fried chicken joints
and dance clubs and night clubs and parks
and lakes and pools and they climb the trees and they drive through town
with their windows down,
their speakers up, volume and the volume of the earth filling itself up,

115

with green, white, pink, yellow, purple, blossom
and spring, they come out into the garden, and weed what they would not have grow there,
they walk in the warm night, hand-in-hand with devil,
they walk side-by-side through the low fog of another May morning.
Sikeston, MO, my hometown, and Lambert's Café.
Fried okra and hot rolls, thrown across the large room,
covered in down-home relics and license plates, the memory of these fifty states
all over, the state flags, the brown paper thrown on the table,
sorghum molasses, turnip greens, the #1 place in America to pig out.
We gnaw on hog jowl and bite into fried catfish.
It is the season to eat what is fresh again, what grows again,
to shed the winter coat for the movement of the foot, the feet walking around
the old neighborhood, swinging in the old swings,
the downtown and the memory of all it used to be, all it is not,
nostalgia and nostalgia and what is missed and what is not,
not that anything is gone, just that everything is,
or everything has changed, a change for the better,
a turn for the worse, an afternoon on the porch drinking coffee
and feeling the breeze pulled through,
the architecture of old homes,
the port-hole windows in the closets upstairs to let the light in,
and the light cometh, it escapes through the clouds,
rays of the good lord, rays of the good sun,
rays of something like a beacon, something that beckons,
that giant tower in the sky guiding us home.
Four days and four temperatures, four places, four people
and this the fourth poem in a series of four seasons.
Take numbers to mean what you will, but as you take them, as you hold them up
to the light, hole them away in your change purse,
write them again and again in your bank book,
recognize them on the headstone, know that they mean something,
they are relevant somehow, as is everything, as is this
dialogue we keep up, as is this you and I.
Dogtown, St. Louis, and we sit on the back patio at Seamus McDaniel's
and wait for something to happen, waiting this time for my sister's child
to enter the world, welcome young girl,
you have sprung in the spring into a bright and blinding and vast and momentous future.
It is the future we are concerned with.
The present is here, and it is so good right now, so green,
so lush, it is the unknown we fear,
the parts of each other we fear, the fear we fear,
what that fear might do to a person, what time might do to a person,
what one season might do, one year, but this is the season
to return to, to be in, this is the season, like all seasons, to live in,
to fill up the hours of the day with laughter and love,

116

hope and worry, pain and longing for what's out there, what's next,
what's better to ignore until it sprouts from the ground,
and then we will watch it, then we will pay attention,
and nourish it so that it flowers, nourish it so that it gives fruit, nourish it
so that it goes to seed and gives back to the ground
all the care we have given to it, I am a gardener of the world,
we are the gardeners of everything,
we plant, we harvest, we fill up the hours between
with good food, good music, drinks and dancing and all good things,
with family, with friends, with the eternal with of everything,
the width between two people, the width two people create side-by-side, together
and out into the shadow and the sunshine.
I know not where I will go next.
I know not what, exactly, to say.
I have been in a place for a long time and I am breaking out of that place,
I am changing, as on the mulberry tree the fruit now grows,
I am the green sway, I am the tall grass,
the small tick in the tall grass as it bites into my hand,
below the glove, above the wrist,
I am blood and water and food and fed,
I am life and death,
and in this moment, I am spring.
Such bold things to declare on a Friday.
I should be struck down, and I have been struck down.
But today, I rise up.
Tomorrow, the Preakness Stakes.
The gamble continues,
the race keeps running, and there is a horse out there
with my number, my name, there is a hope
I refuse to let go.
Whatever optimism is, it is, today, the stuff I am made of.
And of summer ale and pepperoni pizza and bagel and egg and vitamin
and juice and water and coffee and menthol cigarette.
I am these things I take into myself,
I am the pepper plant that takes in the sulfur of a match-tip,
the crab grass that takes in the Roundup,
the barbed-wire that takes in the scissortail flycatcher,
and the scissortail that takes in the flies and mosquitoes at early dusk,
swooping just above the grass in the pasture.
And you, this is what you are to me:
reader, friend, lover,
mother, father, brother, sister,
you are the light in my window, the tall grass below the flies,
the metal post, the car's muffler, you are the spring,
you are the everything, the exit sign,

the Interstate, the 35 and the 44,
the 55 and the 40, you are the number,
the number one, the part of which we are all part,
you are the person I place my faith in.
And outside, now, it is the chapel, the steeple,
the cathedral and the schoolhouse.
The sun shines today, and there's not a cloud in the sky.
Not that clouds mean darkness, except that they do.
Not that rain means weeping, except that it does.
The power plants puts out white tufts of steam, and so these are the clouds
we give back, the water we give back,
even as I shake off in the shower, and watch as it trickles down the drain.
A water treatment plant, and in the old concrete troughs they keep
giant goldfish. The fish come up to the top now,
they take the bait, the worm, the cricket,
I take the bait, and you, hook, line, and sinker.
My horoscope for today suggests something exotic.
My palm suggests a place where the life and heart line meet.
My mind runs across the top of my hand and breaks like a forkéd tongue.
Silver butter knife and spoon and fork.
A wax paper bag, a silver napkin dispenser, and outside, in the park,
the young couple picnics.
It is a good idea, today, an idea not my own,
even though I understand that perhaps no idea is singular,
none individual, I will hold on to some of the older methods of thinking
forever. I will hold on to love forever.
I will hold on to you forever.
I will hold on to the spring, hold on to the goodness,
the evilness, the righteousness and the humbleness,
humble next to the bumble of the bumble bees just outside,
out my window, inside my wall, fighting to get back to the hole I closed.
So time is a portal and sometimes
we fall right through it.
Sometimes yesterday, sometimes tomorrow,
sometimes we fall right into our present moment, déjà vous,
so that we might see ourselves as we actually are for a minute,
we might be able to recognize that we are exactly where we're supposed to be,
exactly who we're supposed to be, and with who, and where, and when,
as we fill up a moment the way the freshly picked wildflowers
fill up the old vase on your desk, your kitchen table,
your kitchen window where the birds hop outside and look in.
When this is all done, I will go on,
and you will go on, but neither of us will be exactly the same,
and we will not go on without each other,
we will never be without each other again,

never without, I will write the future on this morning
because I fear the future, because I know the future knows me better than I him,
or her, because tomorrow I will wake up with you in my arms.
Already the first signs of summer, so early, so late.
Already the sno-cone shops, already the boats pulled out of storage, let down
in the docks, already the revision of everything with which this thing
began, with which we began, you and I, before we knew each other
as we do now, before we saw the cycle, and before we saw now as we do
the cycle as it begins to cycle back, to turn in on itself, the snake at its tail,
may it be unbroken, by and by, lord, by and by.
Friday night and the first of the carnivals begins to spin
in the parking lot of a new strip mall.
We take our time, we rush,
we dizzy and we dizzy again.
The traveling carnival, its goal, method:
feed them, then get them dizzy, then take their money
with whatever games look easy, on the surface, to win.
And so much of it does look easy on the surface.
A bicycle where the steering wheel turns everything opposite,
if the rider could just understand the opposite nature of things,
understand the universe in reverse, backwards,
understand that first feeling of losing the training wheels and rolling
down the street, understand that from the other side of the road,
the front of the bike, understand that and carry that out
and then a new iPod is theirs.
It is not that easy to rewrite history, not that easy to plug in
to the two wires connecting the ears
to a small white box. Not that easy for me, sometimes, to give in
to technology, cell-phones, I can be grumpy
and moan and wail like a tired old man sometimes.
So the rides spin in circles, and even within those circles, circles
that spin on their own, a constellation of spinning
and laughing and smiling and holding hands.
Maybe we're all getting ripped off,
but we're happy about it,
and it's worth every penny, worth the second dollar
I put into the skee-ball machine, to win some giant pink pig
with a sinister smile—he knows what the carny knows,
what I know, what we all know and can thus put behind us
and move on into recognition and human interaction
move on into the next ride, the deep white bucket
of the Ferris wheel.
And from there we see parts of the town we have never seen before.
A caramel apple, and cold soda, a corndog,
and the best show in town tonight, better than any of the movies lit

on the marquis down the street.
The Ferris wheel, named after George Washington Gale Ferris,
the name that goes around itself,
a railroad and bridge-builder,
that first wheel that held 2,000 people, all breathless, all high
in the sky, until it was retired as machines often are,
pulled apart in pieces and used to build a bridge
across the Kankakee River, not too far from its Chicago home.
Sweet home Chicago, Memorial Weekend,
and we drive to the Chautauqua Hills Blues Festival
in Sedan, KS.
And the town sign driving into Main Street: Home of World Famous Clown
Emmett Kelly. Emmett Kelly, who created the first hobo clown,
Weary Willy, a tragic figure who, when sweeping up the ring
after the other acts, would try without success to sweep up the light
that the spotlight made on the ground, even as it moved away,
even as it lasted. A hobo clown doll, named Harley Ledo,
used to sit on the bookcase and look out at me,
a replica of Weary Willy, who was a replica of Emmett Kelly,
who was a replica of America in the depression, a replica
of Sedan, KS, such a small and pretty place to sit in a tent while it storms
outside, such a strange place to find the longest yellow-bricked road
in the world. So a storm comes,
as storms do in southeast Kansas, and the first night's show
moves from a courtyard, the smell of honeysuckle opened-up
and thick, to an old movie theater, a place that was likely
working as hard as Emmett Kelly
during the depression to cheer people up, to give them a place
and a space and darkness and moving light
to escape to, and we escape there, with all these people,
local people, people like us
from the outside world, we escape into the theater
with a bag of cold beer and a small bottle of some syrupy
schnapps, we listen, we tap feet, we take on the surreal
nature of an audience in a surreal setting,
a surreal woman with a hat on playing the blues,
crawled out of a beat-down sedan minutes before,
Sedan, KS, the place where sedans go to die,
where they return to themselves, the homeland of the weary
Buick and Lincoln and Oldsmobile.
Sometimes a theater reveals itself as a theater,
as a history, as a spectacle and it is when this happens,
and when it happens well, that the nature
of the human folds back
on himself, herself,

you go back into a place inside you,
a place that, first seeing the dogwood blossom in March,
first seeing the tulip push up,
first seeing the bee buzz and the bee sting,
first seeing the honeysuckle vine go green,
then red, then white into sweetness,
feels a deep trembling inside somewhere, a deep trembling
to the sound of a guitar and nothing else
inside a movie theater,
a deep trembling at the deep trembling in another's voice,
an authentic trembling there, something real,
something painful, singing
Life is pain, and beautiful as such,
Life is beauty, and painful as such,
the weary blues echo on and out into the lobby,
they walk down the yellow-bricked road,
and stop somewhere near the edge,
they take a heavy breath,
they take a long look around,
they open their hearts and step into tomorrow.
Tomorrow brings lawn chairs and tents and ticks on the dog,
the dog on the Frisbee, a drunk woman
from OK City feeding him crackers,
music on the stage, people all around becoming the stage
as we watch them, and listen, and wait for the darkness
to dance. Tomorrow brings a new job,
painting the exterior of houses,
summer work, at the end of this spring,
something to occupy my hands, my time, as my mind wanders
with the paint chipping to the concrete,
the paint coming down for the new paint to come on,
white and gray and beige and all the dull pale correspondences
of garden homes stacked on each other like moving boxes,
a small golf course and fairway nestled in the rear,
a deck to grill on and watch the white balls move across the day.
Sunburned from the work, I sit this Sunday morning
with a Guinness and hangover,
I sit thinking about you, I am fully here,
you are gone somewhere across America,
I miss you as someone misses the flowers the deer have eaten,
I miss you as someone misses yesterday,
depending on what yesterday it was,
I miss you as someone misses their mother,
their father, their family,
I miss you as the young buck first misses his antlers,

even as he breaks them off against a cold tree.
Sunday morning, and the spring winds down
into the summer, the heat of the summer
has already taken over here—90 degrees
from here on out, 100 degrees looming in that bright and burnt future.
But the rain maintains.
The storms come nearly every night,
they crack the open windows even more open,
they crack the green open,
they crack the crickets open,
everything open and waiting for the water
to return, the water to come back down, the rain,
vitality, wealth of the prosperous gray.
You are away from me, so I call you back.
You are away from me, so I write.
We are watching this together, we are two different places
occupying the same space, the same heart,
held as long as we can stand to hold it,
we are eternal and vernal and one spring
that will one day be mistaken for another spring,
spring as it starts in the soul,
spring as it ends on the skin,
spring as bounty,
spring as beauty,
spring as the truth that castrates itself from the past or present or future,
spring as the moment when the squash blossoms open
in the morning, the moment unseen,
the growth unseen, the magic
that happens when you turn your back.
Back in Kansas the field of the blues grows thick and dense,
with no need to bush-hog, they wait for the day
when it is time to bail the hay.
Outside town I drive down section line roads with the dog,
drinking beer, listening to music, we take our time
and look out at the small plots of wheat
going thick and good, almost too good
from the rain, it is time to cut,
but Sunday, and the hardest job for a farmer
is coming to terms with how to keep the Sabbath holy.
So I take up my glass.
I paint the houses with beautiful gardens,
I paint a three-car garage
to make it look more like the other three-car garages,
I work off the books and get paid hard cash every Friday.
I have not worked like this in a while,

and I lie about my background, my future,
I am just a student looking to make some money,
which is partially true,
but I am also looking for something to occupy my body,
my time, I am looking to cover something up,
I am looking for structure,
I am looking for god, for the feel of the sun
on my calves, the back of my neck,
I am looking for the road to Damascus paved in gold,
the fountain of youth,
the past as it unfolds into a hundred stories, a hundred men, women,
I am looking for the future and where I will be in that future,
where we will be, how we will read this spring
and think of how long ago that seems,
how long a year seems, how long life seems,
I am looking for the seam between fact and fiction,
truth and reality, the seam between two worlds,
two people, as I take my hands and tear at that seam,
pulling the strings out, ripping it open,
taking the fabric apart for you to sew me a quilt
of honesty, love, benevolent deception, bodies, ghosts, the words
and the word as it manifests something real,
something beyond an arbitrary system,
something beyond systems altogether, the word
as it means something purely and exactly and wholly.
You would call me a romantic.
I would call you aromatic.
The morning smells of the first cut grass wet again,
it smells of growth, it smells of you
in the more tender spots
of the house,
the yard, it smells of shit
the dog has rolled in to cover up his own smell,
it smells of the white tail
of the deer bucking away into the distance.
I can sense the end of this thing,
and in seeing it I can sense that there is no end,
that this story will go on a long time after,
after me, after you, I can sense
eternity in the mulberry
as it ripens, falls, rots, and gives way to the summer.
On the highways the animals rot,
the vultures feed, and all over the small birds
are running the poor crows off,
pecking them in the air with a constancy

that resembles war, or fear, or desire.
Last week I watched as a small bird was pecked in the chest,
stunned and bleeding on the barbed wire,
too much in shock to fly away
as I approached, even as I petted its gray coat,
and I believe that the brain
of the small animal is not so different
than the brain of the large animal,
that sometimes reality, naturalism, etc.
is too much to deal with, too much to acknowledge
as we settle into a routine of safety and food and cyclical rain and harvest.
The earth is not that kind.
It is not that kind of place.
It is kind of like the most perfect thing in the world,
as it is the world, and dangerous when it needs to be,
growing when it needs to be,
it is good to be reminded we are inconsequential, it is good to be reminded
we are everything, we are consequence itself,
it is good to take the recycling to the dumpsters,
it is good to take something broken
and start over, to mend, to rot, to give in to the birth of another day
as it draws me one day nearer to you,
to us, one day nearer to everything I dare not try to know.
The last of the spring days now,
and the wind is coming in hard from the south, promising the storms
that will forecast and foreshadow the dry and dull heat of August.
Mosquitoes along the wall,
and I spend the day putting new paint over old paint,
primer on bare wood.
A house with a new coat, such a good thing to see,
as it shakes itself out from the old chips,
the old boards, the old siding, and into something new
and protective and water resistant,
and beautiful.
The man I work with brings a small copperhead
to show me from his minivan, a pregnant snake,
kept in a goldfish bowl with a lid taped to the top.
Its tail is green, and we wonder if this is a signal of the babies to come
or perhaps bait to lure something in.
The spring is still green now, and lush, not yet giving in
to the brown grass of summer.
We pull out our tools from the minivan,
nestled between antique bass lures, bamboo spears,
and other nick-knacks he likes to collect in his spare time.
In the neighbor's yard they keep their car

parked, a doughnut on the back passenger side, so many cars
all over the world right now needing a spare.
A spare and a spear and the fish comes out of the water flopping,
they never give up, even after an hour on shore I've seen a bass
slowly fight to bounce one more time back into the water,
back into his home, as if he can sense where it is even though his eyes
face the sky, as if he can smell the life that place gives off.
The forecast calls for heavy weather tonight,
and so the water will come again,
as it always does, as a constant, as the life-giver and the destroyer of lives
these days—tornadoes and hurricanes
and the great blistering storms that tear a house apart,
turn a car inside out,
take an old barn and park it in the lot down the road a ways.
The water does not lie.
Make no mistake about this.
Let go of it, and you die. Let go of it,
and the life goes out of you, the flop goes out of you
as even the strongest fish cannot survive on land forever.
So take it in its cold forms.
Take it in its spring forms—wet, thick, heavy,
drops dripping and hail making dents in every automobile outside.
Insurance? I've never heard of such a thing.
You wait for the world to show you something, and then you follow
your heart, you follow it to the lake down the street,
I follow it with you, we follow them together
and together we meet, hovering around the same heart,
a bright light shining and humming and playing music inside like a jukebox
beside the water, as if it crawled out of the water,
as if it fell from the sky and found first
and foremost what is best in the world,
what is all in the world,
as we found those things, and held them between us
together. I sit and look out the window
and realize there is no way to end this,
there is, in fact, no end.
So it will never end.
I will go on, and the seasons will go on,
and the rain will come tonight and fill up the sky with cracking thunder
that will scare the dog to my side.
With a little help, we can see this as the perfect thing.
With a little help, and hope, and struggle, and desire
we can get through anything.
Call me what you will, but I will return
to the summer when it comes again,

and the fall, and the winter, and the spring.
I will return in another form,
I will return as the water,
as a man in love, as a lover, a father, as my brother, a fountain
of everything I take
from the seasons, everything I take within
and hold there in my memory, or rather set them free,
like the babies kept in the belly
of a pregnant snake kept in the belly of a fishbowl,
I will let it all out, I will let my life out,
let it move down the ruts
the rain moves through, ruts being only the sign of erosion,
erosion being only the sign that the water
is going somewhere, and that is has a course,
and a destination, and a journey back
to itself. Through you
I have journeyed back to myself, I have become
myself again, that part of me
I can't describe, that part that others may not even believe
exists. But believe.
Believe like the house believes the new paint will make it spring to life again,
believe like the spring believes the water will fill its soul.
Believe that if you start this book again,
the summer will come back,
believe that everything in life will come back
and find you again, that I will find you again,
even when you are far away from me
I will come to you in a dream, or in thought, or in quiet.
And you, you are my seasons, all of them,
you are the constant and the ebb and flow
of the tides that take the water back, that move it all over
the world.
Nothing will be the same after this.
The seasons come and go, they change
the earth every year forever, they have changed you and I, this year,
forever. And so in a land of forevers I pledge my forever to you.
I pledge my baptism in the lake's edge.
I pledge my corndog.
I pledge my tick bite.
I pledge all the things I have pledged throughout, and more.
Spring, you have blossomed.
Your bloom, your storm-swept lady.
I pull a blister from my skin, and wait for the tenderness beneath to heal.
I pull off my sunburn and let the peels loose to the wind.
And the wind takes it, it takes it all,

and paint chips, and golf balls, and small birds and large birds and the leaves of trees
in a thousand directions, it swirls upward with a kindness in where it is going,
a pulse as the gusts come in, and in, bringing the storm at last,
bringing the water,
bringing the next season, the next year,
the next place to live, the next struggle, the next day of doing nothing
but holding each other in the sunlight.
It brings the rest of our lives,
it brings everything,
it brings you home to this place where you belong.

Made in the USA
Lexington, KY
21 June 2010